Romanticism

Published by

THE UNIVERSITY *of* TULSA
University School

TULSA, OKLAHOMA

© 1998 University School. First Edition, 1998. Reprinted 2008, 2016.
All rights reserved. Individual teachers who purchase this book are welcome to make copies for their own classes. Entire schools and districts who wish to use the series may purchase books at bulk rate. Making copies from one book for multiple classrooms or schools is prohibited.

ISBN Number: 1-893413-05-5

Manufactured in the United States of America

All proceeds from this series go to University School at The University of Tulsa, a non-profit educational organization.

SAILS titles include: *Classical Greece*
                                 Ancient Rome
                                 The Renaissance
                                 Baroque & Rococo
                                 Neoclassicism
                                 Romanticism
                                 Ancient Eqypt
                                 Middle Ages

Additional information is available about SAILS materials and University School.

Contact: University School at The University of Tulsa
              800 South Tucker Drive, Tulsa, Oklahoma 74104
              Phone: 918-631-5060   Fax: 918-631-5065
              Visit: 326 South College Avenue, Tulsa, Oklahoma 74104
              e-mail: debra-price@utulsa.edu

The University of Tulsa does not discriminate on the basis of personal status or group characteristics including but not limited to the classes protected under federal and state law in its programs, services, aids, or benefits. Inquiries regarding implementation of this policy may be addressed to the Office of Human Resources, 800 South Tucker Drive, Tulsa, Oklahoma 74104-9700, 918-631-2616. Requests for accommodation of disabilities may be addressed to the University's 504 Coordinator, Dr. Tawny Taylor, 918-631-2315. To ensure availability of an interpreter, five to seven days notice is needed; 48 hours is recommended for all other accommodations. TU#14128

The SAILS Curriculum concept and ideas were developed in conjunction with a grant from the U.S. Department of Education, Javits Gifted and Talented Students Education Grants Program; Award Number R206A990007 for the period January 1999 through January 2003; in the amount of $645,000.

Acknowledgements

Many thanks to Susan Coman and her staff at Protype Inc., Tulsa, Oklahoma, who produced the series. Also thanks to copy editors Katie Abercrombie, Robyn Bowman, Ekta Gupta, Kim Harper, and Andrea Sharrer for the countless hours donated to this project.

Artwork courtesy of Photodisc, Artchives, clip art, and Patricia Hollingworth. Any omission of acknowledgement is unintentional.

Preface

University School teachers created SAILS for students of all ages. SAILS is based on active interdisciplinary learning in a content-rich environment as used at University School. University School at The University of Tulsa is a school for gifted children from preschool through eighth grade. The active interdisciplinary learning approach presented in SAILS enables gifted behaviors to emerge in students in both regular and special classrooms.

The purpose of SAILS is to provide a framework for understanding historical patterns which is often omitted in world, national, and art history courses. This framework is developed by showing modern day links to ancient Western civilizations, presenting reoccurring patterns in history, and acquiring an understanding of the basic ideals of these cultures. Every community in America has visual reminders of ancient civilizations which go unrecognized. Students of all ages can learn to recognize and appreciate this heritage.

SAILS was created by

Editor and Illustrator - Patricia L. Hollingsworth, Ed.D.

Writers and Teachers

Katie Abercrombie	Marilyn Howard
Sharon Block	Cyndie Kidwell
Debi Foster	Gina Lewis
Cathy Freeman	Alicia Parent
Kim Harper	Marti Sudduth

Patricia Hollingsworth

Contents

TIMELINE OF WESTERN CIVILIZATION
Compare Ideals, Art, Architecture 6

WELCOME TO ROMANTICISM
Introduction by Delacroix 9
Romantic Period 1800-1850 11

QUICK FACTS / 12
Romantic Trivia 15

IDEALS
Neoclassicism and Romanticism Compared 16
Architecture 17
Compare and Contrast Architecture 19
How to Write a Paragraph 20

DAILY LIFE
Daily Living in Victorian London 21
The Victorians and Their Homes 23

ROMANTIC ARTISTS / 25
Goya's *The Third of May* 26
Goya's *Cudgels* 28
John Constable 29
Constable's *White Horse* 30
J.M.W. Turner 31
Theodore Géricault 32
Eugéne Delacroix 33
Albert Bierstadt 34
Rosa Bonheur 35
Questions About Romantic Artists 36
Rosa Bonheur's Life 37
Events in the Life of Rosa Bonheur 39
Rosa Bonheur - Write and Imagine 40
Let's Really Look at a Painting: Goya's *Colossus* 41

WRITERS
William Wordsworth 43
Samuel Taylor Coleridge 45
William Blake, Poet and Painter 46
Blake: The Artist 48
Blake: *The Ancient of Days* 49

  Romanticism = Imagination 50
  Romanticism = Fairy Tales 51
  Edgar Allen Poe 54
  Romanticism vs. the Industrial Revolution 55
  Romantic Haiku Poetry 56

MUSIC
  Music in the Romantic Period 57
  Questions About Romantic Music 60
  The Romantic Composers 63
  Questions About Composers 66
  Musical Activity. 68
  Bedrich Smetana 68
  Berlioz's Program Music 71

MATH
  Mathematicians and Their Countries 74
  Puzzle of Mathematicians Countries 75
  Famous Mathematicians Word Search. 77
  Leonhard Euler 78
  Driven by the Love of Math. 80
  Famous Mathematicians Timeline 83
  Lagrange and the Metric System 85
  Metric Matching Quiz 87
  Carl Gauss 88
  Two Mathematicians. 89
  Romantic Age Mathematicians Puzzle. 90
  19th Century Computer History 91
  Computer History Questions. 93

SCIENCE
  R.T. Laennec. 94
  Ignaz Semmelweis 95

ROMANTIC INVENTIONS
  Steam Locomotives. 97
  Responses to Great Inventions. 99
  Inventions, Discoveries, and Events Match. 103

REVIEW
  Romantic Period Timeline. 104
  Romantic Evaluation. 105
  Letters Home 106

BIBLIOGRAPHY / 107

TIME LINE

This timeline is a simplified version of time periods. The dates are all approximate and in reality overlap with one another. One country may be starting a time period just as another is ending it. The idea is to provide some guidelines for understanding ideas and influences.

	800BC-350AD	350-1350AD	1350-1600AD
	CLASSICAL • GREEK • ROMAN	**MEDIEVAL/MIDDLE AGES** • ROMANESQUE • GOTHIC	**RENAISSANCE**

IDEALS

- **Classical Greek Ideals:**
  Freedom
  Symmetry
  Balance
  Beauty
  Order
  Dignity
  "Nothing to excess"

- **Classical Roman Ideals:**
  Grandeur
  Power
  Efficiency
  Practicality

- Life is short, difficult
- God all important
- Afterlife all important

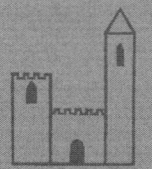

- **Classical Ideals Revived:**
  God and humans important
  Harmony
  Balance
  Beauty
  Order
  Grandeur
  Power

ARCHITECTURE

- **Greek Classical:**
  Parthenon
  Balance, harmony, order

- **Roman Classical:**
  Pantheon
  Technology advancements

- **Romanesque:**
  Fortress-like

- **Gothic:**
  God-like proportion
  Light, airy
  Spires point to God

- **Renaissance Classical:**
  Symmetrical
  Built for God and humans
  Human proportions
  Solid

ART

- **Greeks: Idealistic**
  Classical ideals
- **Romans: Realistic**
  Mythological and
    human subjects
  Classical ideals

- Stiff, heavily draped sculpture
- Cartoon-like drawings
- Biblical subjects only

- Natural and realistic
- Balanced between repose and action
- Biblical, mythological, and human subjects

TIME LINE

1600-1750AD	1750-1800AD	1800-1850AD
• BAROQUE • ROCOCO	NEOCLASSICAL	ROMANTIC

IDEALS

- **Baroque**
  Emotion
  Grandeur
  Energy

- **Rococo**
  Enjoyment
  Pleasure

- **Classical Ideals Revived:**
  Freedom
  Dignity
  Balance
  Beauty
  Order

- Emotion
- Imagination
- Freedom
- Energy
- Turbulence

ARCHITECTURE

- **Versailles:**
  Elaborate
  Grand
- **Palaces:**
  Ornate
  Gold leaf
  Curlicues

- **Monticello:**
  Symmetry
  Balance
  Solid

- **Parliament Houses:**
  Gothic and Medieval

ART

- **Baroque:**
  Emotional
  Swirling
  Dramatic Subject Lighting
- **Rococo:**
  Pretty and Pleasant

- **Classical Ideals:**
  Balance
  Harmony
  Dignity

- Emotional
- Swirling
- Dramatic and exotic
  Lighting
  Subjects

7

Romanticism

WELCOME TO ROMANTICISM

I am Eugéne Delacroix. I believe that painting should be passionate, full of emotion, bursting with energy. They call my paintings "Romantic." I call them LIFE. I am constantly having to contend with Neoclassical painters like David and Ingres whose work reminds me of dead fishes. They say they are painting in the classical style. They make meticulous drawings, but there is no life or passion in their work. Their paintings are like tinted drawings. They never dare to show a brushstroke. It is as if they have no idea what to do with paint. I like my brushstrokes to show. It lets people see the energy that it takes to paint. To me painting and love are alike. Both must have emotion and feeling.

Delacroix

Some people think that I am ill-tempered, but I only want to express my feelings. I have had my fill of Neoclassical architecture with its arches, domes, and pediments. It is so cool, so solid, so rational. Who really believes that is the way humans are? I hope that the Gothic revival style completely takes over architecture. Gothic revival will bring back emotion and passion to architecture. I long to see spires, gargoyles, and pointed arches. I am a great fan of Medieval history.

Gothic style

INTRO

INTRO

We have had enough of rational and reasonable Neoclassicism. Humans are not just intellectual beings. They are also passionate and emotional. We need to return to nature to understand the world. In nature there is a constant and passionate struggle for survival. The Romantic age will be a time for using our emotions and our five senses. It will be an age of sensibility rather than rationality.

Gargoyle

Painted Gothic Arch

Delacroix's
Arab Skirmishing in the Desert

ROMANTIC PERIOD 1800-1850

1. _____ was an artist during the Romantic period.

2. _____ was a reaction to the Neoclassical.

3. _____ painters liked to paint passionately emotional subjects.

4. _____ was a reaction to rational Neoclassical architecture.

5. _____ and _____ are characteristics of the Romantic era.

6. _____ and _____ are characteristics of the Neoclassical.

7. How does Delacroix describe Neoclassical architecture?
_____ , _____ , _____

8. Name two Neoclassical artists.
_____ , _____

ROMANTICISM

WORD BOX

- reason
- Romantic
- rational
- solid
- emotional
- David
- Delacroix
- cool
- Gothic revival
- rational
- passionate
- Ingres
- Romanticism

ROMANTICISM
QUICK FACTS

DATES: 1800-1850 AGE OF SENSIBILITY

Dates for time periods are approximate. In reality most time periods overlap one another.

IDEALS AND VALUES

Passion, emotion, intuition, imagination
Revival of Medieval and Baroque
Reverence for nature
Liberty and social reform

ART

Exotic, violent, legendary, wild animals
Strong contrast
Diagonal composition

Medieval Revival

ARTISTS

1746-1828	Francisco Goya, Spanish artist, evils of society
1757-1827	William Blake, English artist, mystical subjects, poet
1775-1851	J.M.W. Turner, English artist, atmospheric effects
1776-1837	John Constable, English artist, English countryside
1791-1824	Theodore Gericault, French artist, energetic subjects
1796-1875	Eugéne Delacroix, French artist, physical and emotional violence
1822-1899	Rosa Bonheur, French artist, robust nature of animals
1830-1902	Albert Bierstadt, German-born American artist, American West

ENGLISH WRITERS

1770-1850	William Wordsworth, adoration of nature
1771-1832	Sir Walter Scott, glamorized the Middle Ages
1772-1834	Samuel Taylor Coleridge, weird and fantastic, "Ancient Mariner"
1775-1827	William Blake, artist, poet, mystic

Lord Byron

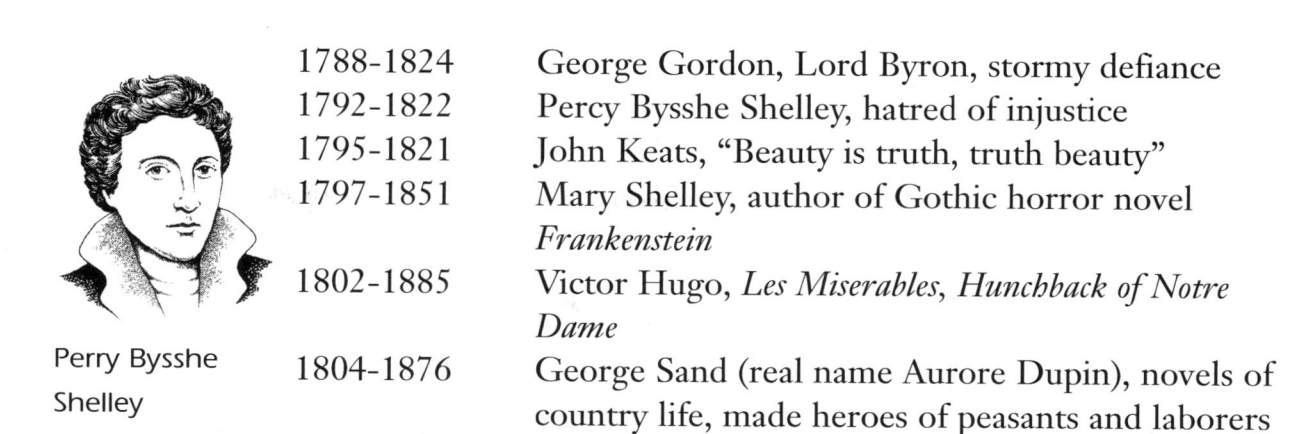

	1788-1824	George Gordon, Lord Byron, stormy defiance
	1792-1822	Percy Bysshe Shelley, hatred of injustice
	1795-1821	John Keats, "Beauty is truth, truth beauty"
	1797-1851	Mary Shelley, author of Gothic horror novel *Frankenstein*
	1802-1885	Victor Hugo, *Les Miserables*, *Hunchback of Notre Dame*
Perry Bysshe Shelley	1804-1876	George Sand (real name Aurore Dupin), novels of country life, made heroes of peasants and laborers

MUSICIANS

1770-1827	Ludwig van Beethoven, chamber music, symphony, passionate idealism, wrote both classical and romantic music, transitional figure
1797-1828	Franz Schubert, music reflects wide range of moods

Franz Schubert

ARCHITECTURE

1753	Writer Horace Walpole begins Gothic style home, Strawberry Hill
1840-60	London Houses of Parliament, Charles Barry and A.W.N. Pugin, Gothic style
1846	Smithsonian Institute built in Gothic style architecture

INVENTIONS, DISCOVERIES, AND EVENTS

1792	Eli Whitney: Cotton gin
1796	Joseph Bramah: Hydraulic Press
1796	Edward Jenner: Smallpox vaccination
1798	Alois Senefelder: Lithography
1799	Rosetta Stone is found
1800	Alessandro Volta: Battery
1802	Sachaus Andreas Winzler: Gas stove
1803	United States buys Louisiana territory from France
1803	Richard Trevithick: Railway locomotive

Steam engine

QUICK FACTS

1804	Napoleon crowns himself emperor of France, the "New Rome"
1807	Gas street lighting
1811	Nicholas Appert: Canned food
1814	Joseph von Frauenhofer: Spectroscope to study spectrum of sunlight
1815	Humphry Davy: Miner's safety lamp
1816	Rene Laennec: Stethoscope
1821	Michael Faraday: Electric motor
1825	First railroad
1826	Patrick Bell: Reaping machine
1827	Joseph-Nicephore Niepce, Louis Daguerre: Photography
1827	Onesiphore Pecqueur: Differential gears
1831	Michael Faraday: Dynamo to produce electricity
1839	Kirkpatrick Macmillan: Bicycle
1840	James Chalmers, Rowland Hill: Postage stamp
1840	Marc Brunel: Interchangeable parts manufacture
1844	Horace Wells: Anesthetics
1844	Samuel Morse: Morse code
1845	R.W. Thomson: Pneumatic tires
1846	Antoine Sax: Saxophone
1847	California gold rush

1839 Bicycle invented

ROMANTIC TRIVIA

1. Name one Romantic architect. _____

2. Name two Romantic musicians. _____
   _____

3. List three characteristics of Romantic art. _____
   _____

4. List four values or ideals of the Romantic era.
   _____
   _____

5. List five artists of this period. _____
   _____
   _____

6. Name six writers of the Romantic era.
   _____
   _____
   _____

7. List seven inventions of this period. _____
   _____
   _____

8. Use the Quick Facts list to find several people whom you want to study. Write their names below and begin to do research on them. Ideas of what to do with your research: Write a poem • create a play • make a book • make a video • write a song • paint pictures • create a dance.

   _____
   _____

Medieval Gargoyle

ROMANTICISM

ARCHITECTURE IDEALS

NEOCLASSICAL AND ROMANTIC COMPARED

	Neoclassical	Romantic
Historical Guide	Classical Greeks	Gothic
	Classical Romans	Medieval
	Renaissance	Baroque
Values and Beliefs	Reason	Emotion
	Logic	Passion
	Rules	Intuition
Art	Simple	Complex
	Calm	Turbulent
Music	Pure beauty	Grand
	Clean basics	Emotional
Architecture	Classical	Gothic
	Renaissance	Medieval

Activity~

Imagine that you are the ruler of a new country. As ruler you must choose between the Neoclassical and the Romantic style for the art, music, architecture, and ideals for your new country.

CIRCLE YOUR CHOICE: NEOCLASSICAL   ROMANTIC

I choose this style because_____

_____

_____

ARCHITECTURE

Gothic Architecture: Notre Dame, Paris

Romantic architecture in the form of Gothic revival never became very popular. Gothic cathedrals with their beautiful majestic spires, rose windows, and flying buttresses had been built to glorify God. In the Romantic period, people tried to manipulate those features for other purposes, but it did not seem to work well. While Romantic art, writing, and music were strong and influential, neo-Gothic architecture waned.

IDEALS

Romanticism: London Houses of Parliament

Romanticism: Neuschwanstein Castle

London Houses of Parliament (1840-60). English architects Sir Charles Barry and A. W. N. Pugin won the competition to build the Houses of Parliament after a fire destroyed the former building. The structure was built in a neo-Gothic style that conveys the feeling of both castle and cathedral.

Castle of Neuschwanstein (1886). This castle was built by the ruler of Bavaria, who was often referred to as "Mad King Ludwig." It is a Romantic fairy tale castle built by a man whose emotions outweighed his intellect. It had no military purpose. It was just a romantic dream built in the Medieval style at great expense. The architect was a theater set designer.

Activity~

IDEALS

What features of Gothic architecture do you like best?

_____

_____

Draw your own example of neo-Gothic style.

COMPARE AND CONTRAST—GRAPHIC ORGANIZER

Study the drawings below of a Medieval castle and Neuschwanstein castle.

Medieval Castle   Neuschwanstein Castle

Look at these buildings. They were built hundreds of years apart! The people in the Romantic time period looked back to the Medieval times for ideas. They copied these ideas, but not completely.

1. In what ways are these two buildings the same?

_____

_____

_____

_____

2. In what ways are they different?

Medieval Castle	Topic considered	Neuschwanstein castle

IDEALS

Medieval Castle

Neuschwanstein Castle

How to Write a Paragraph
Use Your Graphic Organizer

Study the details you wrote about the Medieval castle and Neuschwanstein castle on the graphic organizer on the previous page. Now take this information and turn it into an organized paragraph.

Topic sentence—Your first sentence is the topic sentence. This will summarize your main point of the paragraph. In this topic sentence, state briefly the main ways that the two buildings are both alike and different. Write that sentence now in the space below.

Supporting sentences—These sentences fill in the rest of your paragraph with details that only belong to the subject of your topic sentence. First, in the space below, write all of the details that make the Medieval castle and Neuschwanstein the same. Look at your graphic organizer for ideas. Continue by writing about what makes the two buildings different. Again look at your thinking on the graphic organizer.

Be sure to keep all of your alike ideas together so that they are separated from your different ideas.

_____
_____
_____
_____
_____
_____

ROMANTICISM
DAILY LIVING

DAILY LIVING IN VICTORIAN LONDON

Queen Victoria

Victorian mother and son

Alexandrina Victoria, also known as Queen Victoria, was born during the Romantic era in 1819. She became queen in 1837 and reigned for 63 years. This was the longest reign in the history of England. She was much loved by her subjects and the term "Victorian" has come to describe those years in which she was in power. Let's take a look at life during this time.

If you were poor during this time, you would not go to school. You would probably work for a rich family as a servant. Your duties might be to clean the boots and shoes of the entire household or to light the fires in the numerous fireplaces throughout the house. You would probably sweep floors, clean fireplaces, fill coal scuttles, dust with feather dusters, polish silverware, and collect clothes for the huge daily wash. This was a society where order and cleanliness were valued.

If you were fortunate enough to be born into the upper classes, you would attend a very strict and severe school. The Victorians believed that the disciplines of study and team sports such as rugby and cricket developed the character of future empire builders. If you were a boy, by the age of 12 you would be sent away to boarding school to study Greek, Latin, mathematics, and history to prepare you for Cambridge. Young men in Victorian times had a high calling. It was their responsibility to study hard so that they could carry the benefits of British civilization to all areas of the globe.

Victorian men

Activity~

On the lines below, write five sentences that compare life today to a poor child's life in Victorian England.

_____
_____
_____
_____

On the lines below, write fives sentences comparing life today to a rich child's life in Victorian England.

_____
_____
_____
_____
_____

Would you like to have lived during the Victorian reign? Why or why not?

_____
_____
_____
_____
_____

DAILY LIFE

The Victorians and Their Homes

Adults in Victorian London changed their clothing two to three times a day, always dressing for dinner. A man would wear a shining white shirt with a high stiff collar, a cravat (which is a necktie), trousers, an inner coat called a waistcoat, and an outer coat called a frock coat. A tall black hat topped off this wardrobe, and he was ready for the carriage to carry him to the office.

Victorian women

Victorian man

The lady of the house had a maid to help her dress because it was a strain to tighten the corset down to the 18 inches which was fashionable for the waistline. She would then be buttoned into a full-cut, floor-length dress with puffed sleeves. Underneath all of this were large, figure-hiding petticoats. Because she was a society lady, she did not wear makeup as did the actresses in the theatres. Her long hair was brushed and coiled into a large bun.

The Victorian home was lavishly decorated, and no space was left vacant. They had striped wallpaper covered with large flowers. The walls were covered with paintings, mirrors, engravings, and mottos. The windows were covered with heavy drapes that had lace fringes. The furniture was massive with curved legs and carved armrests. The fireplace mantle was covered with assorted figurines and crystal bowls. Embroidered cloths covered the tables and piano, while potted plants and palms filled in the corners. Collections of wax fruit, shells, butterflies, stuffed birds, photographs, and vacation souvenirs filled any remaining areas. Tassles hung from the

Victorian rooms

Victorian room

doorways, and carpets covered the floors.

Draw a Victorian room. Be sure to add the man and lady of the house.

DAILY LIFE

ROMANTICISM
ARTISTS

Romantic Artists

The Romantic Era. Here the word romantic means adventure. The adventures of Romantic artists included painting and visiting exotic places, recreating Medieval times, exploring new ways to create, and defying rules. Many of these artists were also social misfits. The Romantic period included a good number of artists who fit the "mad genius" stereotype. In modern times we have grown accustomed to associating the "mad genius" with creative artists. This idea developed in the Romantic era.

Artists in the Romantic period were not romantic in the sense we use the word today. They were romantic in the sense that they believed in the importance of emotion and deep feeling. The way this was often shown was with a swirling composition, unusual subject matter, free brush strokes, stark use of blacks and whites, and dramatic colors such as red and black.

Goya's *Colosslus*

Francisco Goya
1746-1828

Goya's *The Third of May, 1808*

Francisco Goya, a Spanish Romantic painter, saw the evil and base side of human life. He experienced Napoleon's troops capturing the city of Madrid. His painting *The Third of May, 1808* shows Spanish loyalists being executed by Napoleon's troops. Goya's paintings often exposed the evils of ignorance and arrogance.

Napoleon had entered and occupied the city of Madrid. Those who fought against him were round up and shot. The painting shows the French soldiers using a lamp so they can more easily kill their frightened and helpless victims.

Activity~

List Romantic characteristics that you see in Goya's art work.
See page 25 for help.

Types of subject matter: _____

_____

_____

_____

Things that are important:

_____

_____

_____

Type of composition:

_____

_____

_____

Describe how this painting makes you feel:

_____

_____

_____

_____

ART

GOYA'S CUDGELS

Goya's art often shows that which frightens people deeply—madness, inhumanity, savagery, hopelessness, and helplessness. His art is full of passion and feeling. You can see it not only in the subject matter but also in his brooding colors and the way he uses the brush. His brush work is loose and dramatic.

The painting below is called *Fight with Cudgels*. It shows two people with clubs beating each other, possibly to death. These people look as if they are both stuck in quicksand. They could most likely help each other out of this situation if they were not in such a rage.

Goya's *Fight with Cudgels*

Activity~

These paintings are from what is referred to as Goya's dark period. Use that term to compare this work to something else.
1. Goya's paintings are as dark as war.
2. Goya's paintings are as dark as_____.
3. Goya's paintings are as dark as_____.
4. Goya's paintings are as dark as_____.
5. Write a poem about Goya's dark paintings.

_____
_____
_____
_____

John Constable
1776-1837

Constable's *Stour Valley and Dedham Church*

John Constable was an English landscape painter who strongly influenced the French Romantics such as Gericault and Delacroix. They admired the subjects he painted and the way he freely put paint onto canvas. People liked the way that Constable used natural green colors for grass and trees. Artists before Constable had used browns and golds.

Constable worked directly from nature, studying light and atmospheric conditions. The painting *Stour Valley and Dedham Church* shows the English countryside. Constable was an artist who made the Romantics honor and revere nature. The outdoors became a symbol of quest and adventure that the Romantics loved.

Activity~

Look at the outdoors where you are and make a drawing of it.

CONSTABLE'S WHITE HORSE

Constable's painting *The White Horse* is another example of the lovely English landscape.

Activity~

Look at Constable's horse and draw one of your own. Look for other pictures or paintings of horses and draw those also.

Joseph Mallord William Turner
1775-1851

Turner's *Rain, Steam, and Speed*

Joseph Mallord William Turner was usually known as J.M.W. Turner. He was an English artist who captured the turbulence and agitation of nature and atmospheric effects. He was fascinated by the wildness of nature, and his work became increasing abstract with the years. His painting *Rain, Steam, and Speed* shows his fascination with the machines and inventions of his time period.

Activity~

Try to create your own atmospheric paintings. You will need small sponges, small rags, and q-tips instead of brushes. Brown paper sacks make good paper. Cut them into several different sizes. Tempera or acrylic paint will work well for your first experiments. Put newspapers under your brown paper sack paper. It is best to work while outside or looking out a window. Experiment to see what works well. Always clean up after you paint.

Theodore Géricault
1791-1824

Géricault's *Mounted Officer of the Imperial Guard*

Theodore Géricault was a Frenchman whose art is the essence of Romantic art. His subject matter was bold and vigorous, as was the way he painted. His horses show all the passion and energy that he felt for them. He lived, painted, and died in the Romantic style. His death was the result of a riding accident.

Activity~

What Romantic characteristics do you see in Géricault's painting?

_____
_____
_____
_____

Eugéne Delacroix
1796-1875

Delacroix's *Arabs Skirmishing in the Desert*

Frenchman Eugéne Delacroix (1796-1875) was a moody, difficult person and a brilliant artist. He painted violent and exotic subjects from the past and the present. His visit to Morocco inspired scenes from a harem. He painted with intense colors and stark color contrasts always striving for the essence of the scene rather than precision or exactitude. One of his most famous paintings, *Liberty Leading the People*, is on French paper money along with a portrait of Delacroix. *Arabs Skirmishing in the Desert* is an example of the excitement and violence often seen in Delacroix's work.

Activity~

What elements of the Romantic style do you see in Delacroix's painting?

_____
_____
_____

Albert Bierstadt
1830-1902

Bierstadt's *Emigrants Crossing the Plains*

Albert Bierstadt (1830-1902), a German-born American painter, captured magnificent panoramas of the American West. Some of his paintings were as large as 9 feet by 12 feet. He was a showman who charged admission to see his paintings which were augmented with potted plants and velvet drapery. He even provided his public with magnifying glasses so they could examine the tiniest of details in his paintings. Bierstadt's *Emigrants Crossing the Plains* shows his love of the American wilderness.

Activity~

Make two lists of what you think the people crossing the plains will face. Make one list about the joys they might experience and one of the hardships.

Joys	Hardships

Tell why you would or would not want to take their journey.

_____
_____

Rosa Bonheur
1822-1899

Rosa Bonheur (1822-1899) was a French woman who loved painting animals. To get excellent sketches for her painting *The Horse Fair*, she disguised herself as a man. That way she was hardly noticed and could get more work done. Her home in Paris was almost like a zoo with animals everywhere.

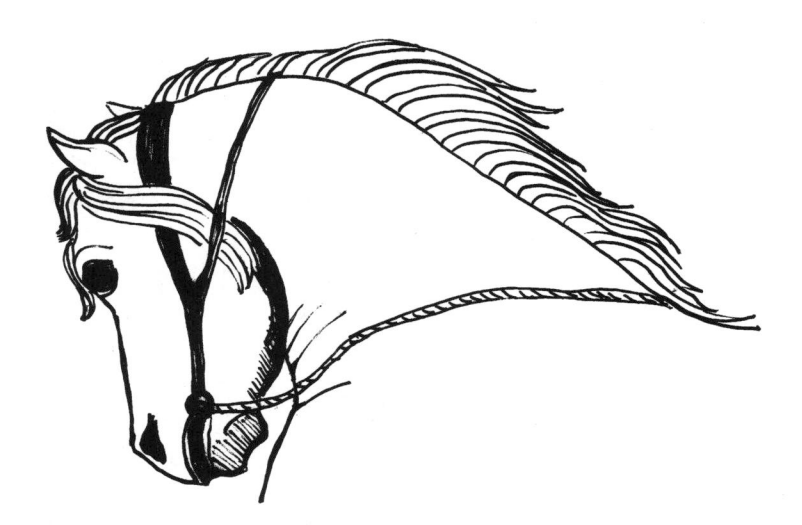

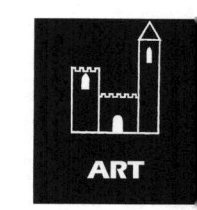

Rosa Bonheur

ART

Activity~

Look at the illustration of Bonheur's horse and draw your own. Continue to look for other illustrations or paintings of horses to draw. The more you practice drawing, the better you will become.

QUESTIONS ABOUT ROMANTIC ARTISTS

1. _____ was the artist who painted *Liberty Leading the People*. His picture and the painting are on French paper money.

2. _____ was the artist who loved and painted animals.

3. _____ was the Spanish artist who painted the evils of society.

4. _____ was the English landscape painter who influenced Delacroix and painted *The White Horse*.

5. _____ painted huge paintings of the American West.

6. _____ painted atmospheric effects of nature.

7. Which Romantic artist do you find the most interesting?
   _____

8. Write as many single words as you can to describe Romantic painting.
   _____
   _____

Activity~

Draw a picture in the Romantic style.

ROSA BONHEUR'S LIFE

On March 16, 1822, a little girl was born in France who would grow up to be one of the most celebrated artists in French history.

Rosa was a happy child. She had two younger brothers, and her father was an artist. Rosa's parents encouraged their children to draw and even let them draw on the walls of their home! Rosa loved animals and her drawings were her mother's favorite works of art.

When Rosa was seven, her family moved to Paris, where Rosa's sister was born. Three years later Rosa's mother died, leaving her father alone to care for four children. Her father hoped that Rosa would someday be able to earn her living as an artist. In those days women weren't encouraged to be artists. Only a few women were well known as artists when Rosa was a girl.

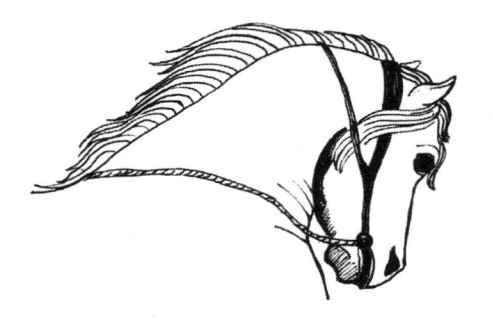

Rosa's father began giving her art lessons when she was thirteen. Every day she had assignments such as drawing flowers or fruit. At fourteen Rosa began going to the Louvre (loo-v), a famous art museum in Paris. There she practiced her skills by copying the paintings she saw. When she returned home each evening, she read French history.

In 1841 Bonheur exhibited her first painting at the Salon, an important art show in France. She was only nineteen. The painting was *Rabbits Nibbling Carrots.* At the age of twenty, Bonheur became even more fascinated with art. She went to fairs to observe the animals. In order to do this, she had to apply for a permit to allow her to wear pants! She studied other artists' paintings of horses and went to butcher shops to cut up portions of animals to see firsthand their anatomy.

Rosa's lion

In 1845 one of Bonheur's paintings won third prize at the Salon. Her work began selling for high prices. Three years later, she won first prize at the Salon for her painting *Cows and Bulls of the Cantal*. Her father's dream had come true. Bonheur would always be able to earn her living with her art.

In 1853 Bonheur's masterpiece *The Horse Fair* was exhibited at the Salon. It was an enormous painting, 8 feet by 17 feet. The painting was so popular that she was asked to bring it to Buckingham Palace for Queen Victoria to see.

With the money she earned, Bonheur bought a chateau (house) in the French countryside. There she kept a zoo full of animals. There were dogs, ponies, deer, elk, horses, sheep, gazelles, bulls, cows, monkeys, a yak, a boar, an eagle, and even a lion! She painted pictures of them all. The lion was her favorite.

In 1865 Rosa Bonheur became the first woman to receive the French Legion of Honor. The emperor refused to present the award to a woman, so the empress presented it instead.

At the age of 67, Bonheur began another wonderful adventure. In 1889 Buffalo Bill and his Wild West Show came from America to Paris. For the seven months the show was in Paris, Rosa was with them. She sketched the horses, bison, cowboys, and Native Americans. She even painted a portrait of Buffalo Bill. He was very happy with the painting and cherished it all his life.

For the remainder of her life, Bonheur painted her beloved animals. In 1899 she became very ill and died. The world was sad to lose her, but her reputation as an artist inspires other artists and continues to reflect her beliefs that nature is always true and beautiful.

Buffalo Bill

EVENTS IN THE LIFE OF ROSA BONHEUR

Below is a list of the events in the life of Rosa Bonheur. They are not in correct order. Please number them in the order in which they occurred.

_____ Rosa Bonheur begins taking art lessons from her father.

_____ Bonheur is born in 1822.

_____ Bonheur wins third prize at the Salon.

_____ Bonheur paints *The Horse Fair*.

_____ Her mother dies.

_____ She goes to the Louvre almost daily to copy paintings.

_____ The Bonheur family moves to Paris, France.

_____ Bonheur receives a permit to wear pants in public.

_____ Buffalo Bill's Wild West Show comes to Paris.

_____ Bonheur dies in 1899.

ROSA BONHEUR—
IMAGINE AND WRITE

Rosa Bonheur's masterpiece is *The Horse Fair*. If you can find a copy of her painting, look at it closely. Try to imagine the sights, smells, and sounds happening in this moment captured by Bonheur. List below words that describe these things.

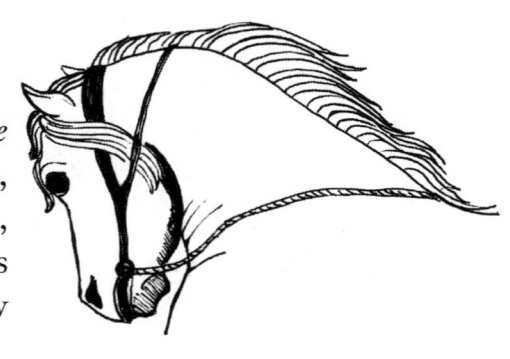

What do I see?	What do I smell?	What do I feel?

Now, use the words you listed above to help you compose a paragraph. Imagine that you are in Bonheur's painting and paint a picture with words. Try to make your paragraph as powerful as the painting.

LET'S REALLY LOOK AT A PAINTING

Study carefully Goya's *Colossus* painting and then answer the following questions.

1. **Subjects**—check what you see

    animals___   buildings___   trees___   sky___   flowers___

    adults___   children___   indoors___   outdoors___   food___

    musical instruments___   transportation vehicles___   other_____

2. **Lines**—check what you see

    sharp____   curved____   choppy___   thick___   thin___

    vertical___   horizontal___   diagonal___   jagged___

    other_____

3. What lines are repeated the most? _____

4. **Shapes**—check what you see

    circles___   squares___   rectangles___   triangles___

ART

41

5. What shapes are **repeated** the most? _____
_____

6. What kind of **balance** is used?
    symmetrical (each side of the painting is similar) ___
    asymmetrical (each side of the painting is different) ___
    radial (subjects branch out like a wheel from a central point) ___

7. **Focal point**—What is the first thing you see in the painting?_____
_____

8. **Purpose**—check what you think is the artist's primary purpose.
    to imitate nature ___
    to express emotion ___
    to show a creative design ___

9. **Describing words**—check the words below that describe this painting.

    strength___   love___   excitement___   courage___   fear___

    hope___   hate___   anger___   loneliness___   sadness___

    peace___   death___   mystery___   happiness___   other_____

10. **Write a paragraph**—Look at the painting one more time. Study your answers to these questions. Then on a separate sheet of paper, write a paragraph describing this artwork and your reaction to it.

For more information on looking at paintings see Hollingsworth and Hollingsworth's *Smart Art* published by Zephyr Press.

ROMANTICISM
WRITERS

William Wordsworth
1770-1850

William Wordsworth

William Wordsworth loved nature. He was called the greatest of the English nature poets. He once said that he deliberately chose to write his poems in "the language of conversation in the middle and lower classes of society." The following few lines are from a sonnet that mourns our world because it has become too materialistic.

WRITING

The World Is Too Much With Us

The world is too much with us; late and soon,

Getting and spending, we lay waste our powers;

Little we see in Nature that is ours;

We have given our hearts away, a sordid boon!

Activity~

1. Explain in your own words the meaning of the line "The world is too much with us." Remember that Wordsworth loved nature.

   _____
   _____
   _____

2. Use your dictionary and look up the words *sordid* and *boon* from the last line of this verse. Write the definitions below. Is a sordid boon a good thing? Yes or No.

   _____
   _____
   _____

3. Wordsworth loved nature and was concerned about what was happening to it when he wrote this poem over 100 years ago. What do you think he would feel if he were alive today? Would he be optimistic about the survival of nature?

   _____
   _____
   _____

4. Write your own paragraph or poem about nature.

   _____
   _____
   _____

WRITING

Samuel Taylor Coleridge
1772-1834

Samuel Taylor Coleridge was a poet who believed that imagination was the ability to create new worlds. He was fascinated with the exotic Orient. Here are a few lines from one of his poems.

Kubla Khan
In Xanadu did Kubla Khan
A stately pleasure-dome decree:
Where Alph, the sacred river, ran
Through caverns measureless to man
Down to a sunless sea.

Coleridge is writing about a place called Xanadu and a ruler named Kubla Khan. Read this stanza and imagine what Xanadu looks like. Draw it below. Try to find the entire poem at your school or city library.

William Blake
1757-1827

William Blake was an artist, a poet, and a self-proclaimed mystic. A mystic is a person who experiences profound spiritual experiences. Blake thought that the human imagination expressed the "Eternal" or God. He believed that humans possessed the virtues of mercy, pity, peace, and love.

Blake published some poetry at the beginning of the French Revolution called *Songs of Innocence*. Blake was optimistic about the revolution because he believed it held the promise of a better life for all people. Following are a few lines from a poem in this collection.

WRITING

The Lamb
Little Lamb, who made thee?
Dost thou know who made thee?
Gave thee life, and bid thee feed,
By the stream and o'er the mead;
Gave thee clothing of delight,
Softest clothing, woolly, bright;
Gave thee such a tender voice,
Making all the vales rejoice?

Blake also published a collection of poems titled *Songs of Experience*. Following are a few lines from a poem in this collection.

The Tiger
Tiger! Tiger! burning bright
In the forest of the night,
What immortal hand or eye
Could frame thy fearful symmetry?
In what distant deep or skies
Burnt the fire of thine eyes?
On what wings dare he aspire?
What the hand dare seize the fire?

These two poems are very much alike and also very different. List three things that are similar, and then list three things that are different.

Similar

1. _____
2. _____
3. _____

Different

1. _____
2. _____
3. _____

Write a sentence explaining how you think Blake felt when he wrote "The Lamb."

_____
_____
_____
_____

Write another sentence explaining how he might have felt when he wrote "The Tiger."

_____
_____
_____
_____

WRITING

BLAKE: THE ARTIST

Romantic artists such as William Blake and Francisco de Goya dealt with difficult themes such as hatred, brutality, and savagery. In the Bible, Adam and Eve's children Cain and Abel have difficulty getting along with each other. Jealousy and resentment build until finally Cain kills Abel. William Blake's painting *The Body of Abel Found by Adam and Eve* shows the grief and horror that is felt when the parents discover Abel's dead body.

WRITING

Blake's *Body of Abel Found by Adam and Eve*

Activity~

What does Blake do to make us see the feelings and emotions of:

Adam _____

Eve _____

Cain _____

What does Blake indicate will happen to Cain?

_____

How does Blake show it?

_____

_____

48

BLAKE: THE ANCIENT OF DAYS

Even though people acknowledge that God is a spirit, some artists have made physical portrayals of the Creator. William Blake's *Ancient of Days* is based on a verse in the Bible in Proverbs in which God "sets a compass upon the face of the deep."

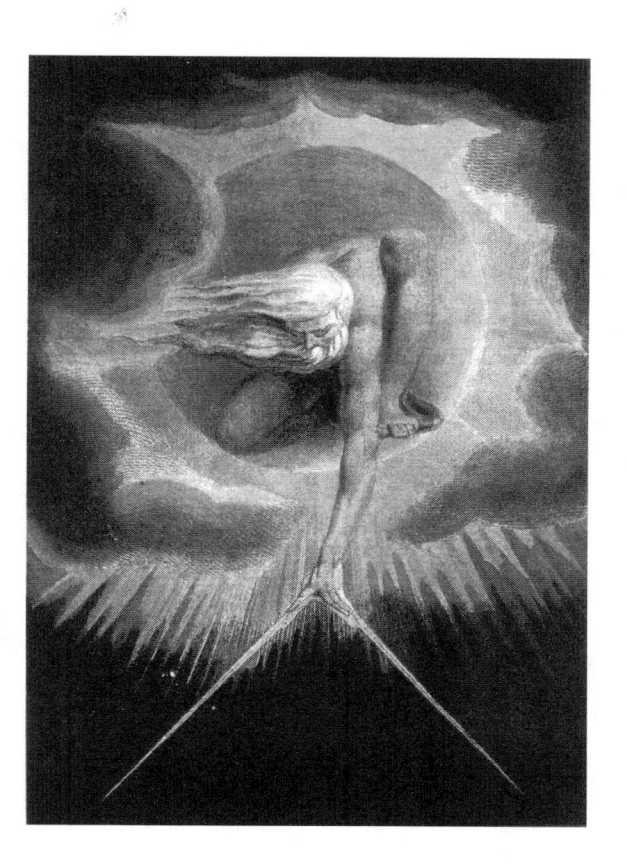

Blake's *Ancient of Days*

Activity~

What do you think Blake was trying to show in this artwork?

_____
_____
_____
_____
_____
_____

ROMANTICISM = IMAGINATION

Listen to this list of words that describes Romanticism:
- emotional
- spontaneous
- free
- imaginative

Now listen to this list of words that describes what Romanticism is not:
- logical
- organized
- factual

Here is a romantic poem about snow. When you read it, ask yourself if snow can talk to people and play with people. Is the poet writing facts about snow, or is he using his imagination?

Soft Snow
I walked abroad in a snowy day;
I asked the soft snow with me to play;
She played and she melted in all her prime,
And the winter called it a dreadful crime.

WILLIAM BLAKE (1757-1827)

In the boxes below, draw snow in a non-romantic, logical way first. Then draw snow in a romantic, creative way.

Logical Snow | **Creative Snow**

ROMANTICISM = FAIRY TALES

Do you remember the story called "Little Snow White" by the Brothers Grimm? It is about a beautiful princess and her jealous stepmother who has a magic mirror that talks. One day the mirror tells the stepmother queen that Snow White is more beautiful than she is. Snow White has to run away in the woods to get away from the angry queen.

Draw a picture of Snow White running away in the woods.

Seven dwarfs let her live in their home, and she is very happy until the queen finds out where she is. The queen disguises herself as an old woman and tricks Snow White into eating a poisonous apple that puts her to sleep.

Draw a picture of the queen giving Snow White the poisonous apple.

The seven dwarfs find Snow White collapsed on the ground. They build her a glass coffin and put her outside on the mountain. One day a prince finds her, she wakes up, and they get married.

Draw a picture of Snow White with her prince.

This fairy tale was popular in the 1800s during the Romantic period. Romantic writers did not like to think about the factories and inventions of their century. They liked to use their imagination to escape the daily routines of cities and business. Romantics especially liked legends about faraway places. That's why stories like this one about Snow White were so popular.

Pretend that you are Snow White. Write five words to describe how you feel running away in the woods.

_____

Now write five more words to describe how you feel taking the apple from the old woman who is really your jealous stepmother queen.

_____

Draw Your Own Fairy Tale Ending. How else could this story about Snow White have ended? Start at your second picture where she gets the poison apple and falls asleep. Now change the ending and use your imagination.

Draw a picture of your new ending.

WRITING

Write about your new ending.

_____
_____
_____
_____
_____

Edgar Allan Poe
1809-1849

Edgar Allan Poe was an American with an international reputation as a critic, poet, and writer of short stories. Poe condemned American materialism and devoted himself wholly to his art. He was the first American to live his life entirely as an artist. Poe's definition of poetry was "the creation of beauty," and he believed that all poetry should appeal equally to reason as well as emotion.

Below is the first stanza of a lyrical poem by Edgar Allan Poe.

Edgar Allan Poe

Annabel Lee
It was many and many a year ago,
In a kingdom by the sea,
That a maiden there lived whom you may know
By the name of Annabel Lee;
And this maiden she lived with no other thought
Than to love and be loved by me.

Romantic Illustration

Activity~

This poem has been described as a lyrical masterpiece which means that it is a musical poem. Do you think this poem has a musical effect? Explain why or why not. Examine the rhythm and the word choice. Notice the use of repeated words and phrases.

_____
_____
_____
_____

Ask your teacher for help if you are interested in knowing what happened to Annabel Lee. You can find the entire poem in books of poetry by Poe.

ROMANTICISM VS. THE INDUSTRIAL REVOLUTION

The Industrial Revolution dominated the 1800s. During this time new machines and inventions were constantly being created. Some of these inventions were train engines, the cotton gin, canned food, bicycles, and the reaping machine. People moved to cities to work in factories. Bigger, stronger, faster—these were the key words for what people called "progress."

The Romantics did not like these changes to their world. They turned away from machines and looked to nature and rural living instead. They wrote about unsophisticated topics and scenery.

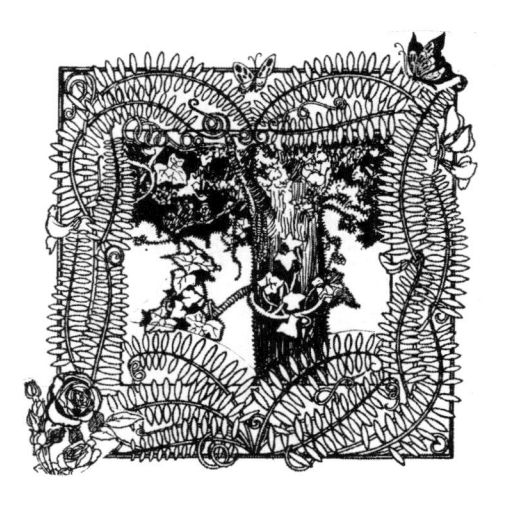

ROMANTICS REJECTED MACHINES AND LOVED NATURE

Go outside and observe a beautiful scene in nature. Draw that scene below.

Romantic Haiku Poetry

Now write down words that describe your drawing.

Adjectives

shape _____

color _____

texture _____

other features _____

Nouns

What things are in my drawing? _____

_____

Verbs

What action do I see? _____

_____

Similes— Use your imagination

This scene is like a _____

_____

Haiku

Haiku poetry is a Japanese poetic structure with three lines and definite syllable counts for each line. Haiku is normally written to describe nature.
Look at the words and drawings of your scene. Close your eyes and feel a sense of music and flowing smoothness.

Now using these ideas, write a three-line unrhymed poem about your scene. The required number of syllables for each line is marked in parentheses.

_____(5)

_____(7)

_____(5)

ROMANTICISM
MUSIC

Music in the Romantic Period

Jean-Jacques Rousseau, political philosopher and writer, inspired the French Revolution in which the French monarchy was overthrown during the Neoclassical period. Rousseau valued personal feelings above the Neoclassical emphasis on the ability to reason. Rousseau valued spontaneity and impulsiveness above the self-control and restraint esteemed in the previous century. Society was changing, and the common man and his feelings were important. A social revolution was taking place along side the Industrial Revolution. In music, composers and musicians revolted against the rules and restraints of the classical era. This movement in the arts is known as the Romantic period which occurred between 1825 and 1900.

Jean-Jacques Rousseau

Composers began to experiment with breaking traditional musical rules. Composers felt free to express their own ideas and feelings about life through their music. They were not obligated to write music to please a patron who paid his salary. Because individualism was highly prized, many different types and styles of music emerged during the Romantic period. But all styles have one thing in common - all music during the Romantic era involved showing emotion.

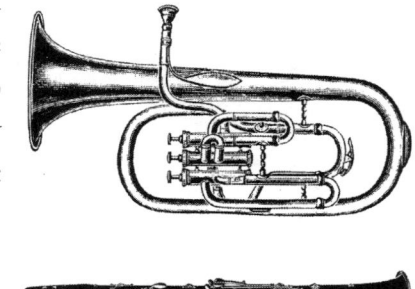

The Industrial Revolution influenced music in many ways. Machinery mechanisms were applied to existing instruments making vast improvements in the musician's ability to play fast and difficult music. New instruments such as the **tuba**, **trombone**, **clarinet**, and **English horn** were added to the orchestra. The piano was improved and enlarged. It became *the* solo instrument of the Romantic era. A machine, the **metronome**, was invented to keep a steady beat and to help the performer interpret what speed the composer wanted his music played.

With the rise of industry, a working middle class emerged. Many people became interested in music and attended public concerts, though their tastes were often unsophisticated. Music critics began to emerge to interpret the music for the public. The business of music emerged during the Romantic era. Composers began to write to please the masses. They needed to sell their music because they had no patron to support them. Composers and musicians wanted to dazzle their audiences with amazing displays of their technical ability. A colorful personality became an asset to selling the music of a composer. Some composers, such as Franz Liszt, had an almost rock star following.

Franz Liszt

The church no longer supported composers, so composers were free to express their own feelings about religion through music. However, this music was not intended to be performed in a church service. Instead, it was performed in a concert hall.

In previous times young musicians were schooled in music through an apprentice method. Teaching music became a profession during the Romantic era. Music research began in universities and conservatories that offered music programs. Students in these schools completed many collections of composer's music from previous times. Felix Mendelssohn, a Romantic composer, found and collected the music of Johann Sebastian Bach, the great baroque composer. The works of Beethoven and Mozart were also collected and published.

Felix Mendelssohn

Many music teachers were also composers. These teacher/composers wrote **etudes**, works for instruments to help their students develop their technical expertise for the new challenging music being written.

Romantic composers exercised musical freedom in many different ways. **Chromaticism**, using the 1/2 step intervals not included in major or minor scales, was used extensively to free the rigid tonal structure found in classical music. Phrases became irregular and imbalanced, something unheard of in the classical period.

Richard Wagner

Franz Liszt

Music in the Classical period was light and clear. Music in the Romantic period was heavy and complicated. Composers tried unusual combinations of instruments to make interesting new sounds. Solo songs with piano accompaniment were written expressing the feelings and ideas of the composer.

Many new and individual styles emerged in the Romantic era. Some composers wrote **program music**. This is music written to tell a story, create a musical picture, or imitate the sounds of nature. A whole orchestral composition written without a specific form and using a musical "program" was called a **symphonic poem**. In a symphonic poem, the program or story defines the form of the music. A rise of patriotism and pride in country, called **nationalism**, led to the composition of music with national themes such as folk songs and musical descriptions of the country. Patriotic music became popular. The **waltz** became a leading style for dancing. **Ballet**, **opera**, and **operetta**, a lighter form of opera, were immensely popular.

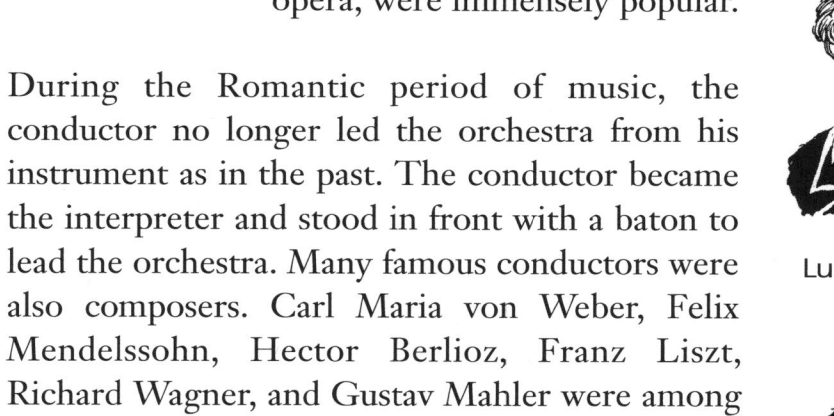

During the Romantic period of music, the conductor no longer led the orchestra from his instrument as in the past. The conductor became the interpreter and stood in front with a baton to lead the orchestra. Many famous conductors were also composers. Carl Maria von Weber, Felix Mendelssohn, Hector Berlioz, Franz Liszt, Richard Wagner, and Gustav Mahler were among those famous conductor/composers.

Ludwig van Beethoven

Many composers of the period were also **virtuosos**, highly skilled musicians. Some composer/virtuosos were Niccolo Paganinni on violin and pianists Franz Liszt, Ludwig van Beethoven, and Frederic Chopin.

Frederic Chopin

Questions About Romantic Music

What political philosopher and writer inspired the French Revolution?

When did the Romantic period of music take place?

What were some of Jean-Jacques Rousseau's ideas?

Write two sentences in your own words that compare Rousseau's ideas to the ideas popular in the Neoclassic (classical, in music) period.

How did musicians and composers adopt the ideas of the Romantic era?

Jean-Jacques Rousseau

List six ways the Industrial Revolution influenced music.

How did a musician get his training before the Romantic period?

How did a musician get his training during the Romantic period?

What benefit of the musical research done during this period do we have today?

List six ways Romantic composers exercised their musical freedom.

_____
_____
_____
_____
_____
_____

Define the following.

- program music _____
- symphonic poem _____
- nationalism _____
- waltz _____
- operetta _____
- virtuoso _____

How did the role of the conductor change in the Romantic period?

_____
_____
_____
_____

Draw a picture of one of the composer/virtuosos on page 59 conducting an orchestra.

WHAT DO YOU THINK?

How were the composers of the Romantic era similar to today's rock star?

_____
_____
_____

Franz Liszt

Based on your knowledge, how is the music industry of the Romantic period similar to the music industry of today?

_____
_____
_____

Romantic era audiences loved Franz Liszt's music, and he had many faithful admirers. Listen to *Les Preludes* by Liszt.

Compare this music to a CD of a modern rock star. List many ways these two are different.

_____
_____
_____
_____

How are they the same?

_____
_____
_____
_____

MUSIC

The Romantic Composers

The common element in the music of the Romantic period was the display of emotion. Composers tried to develop their own individual and unique styles reflecting the cultural values of the 19th century — the importance of feelings and individualism, the rise of the common man, personal freedom, and nationalistic pride in country. Three great composers lived and worked in Paris, the cultural center of the Romantic period. **Franz Liszt**, **Hector Berlioz**, and **Frederic Chopin**, friends and geniuses, developed very different styles but reflected romantic ideals in their music.

Frederic Chopin

Franz Liszt

Franz Liszt, composer and the greatest virtuoso pianist of the Romantic era, was born in Hungary in 1811. His father, a gifted amateur musician, taught young Liszt to play the piano beginning at age five. Liszt began to compose when he was eight and perform as a concert pianist at age nine. His father took his prodigy son to Vienna where he studied with Karl Czerny, one of Beethoven's students, and Antonio Salieri. Young Liszt even met the legendary Beethoven.

Franz Liszt

Liszt contributed greatly to the music of the Romantic era. As the first person to give completely solo recitals, he encouraged the performance of music of the masters from past eras. He mentored rising composers, taught other virtuosos, and wrote books about Romantic music. He invented the **symphonic poem** for orchestra, a piece in one movement that describes something or tells a story. He invented **transformation of themes**, a technique that takes one or two musical themes or ideas, alters them, and uses them as a foundation for an entire piece. His piano compositions reached new heights of technical virtuosity and had a thick, rich, nearly orchestral sound.

Liszt's compositions helped shape the future of music as well. He extended and developed the use of **chromatic harmony**, which foreshadowed the breakdown of tonality and led to 20th century atonality.

Hector Berlioz

Born in 1803 in France, Hector Berlioz's early musical training was in flute and guitar. This early training shaped the way he approached composition. Liszt and Chopin composed first from the piano and then orchestrated the music into the various instruments. Berlioz conceived of the music in orchestral form.

Hector Berlioz

Berlioz came to Paris to study medicine, but instead entered the Paris Conservatoire to study composition. His music and his life were full of passion and inner fire. He had a deep interest in literature from which he received inspiration to express literary stories and themes through music.

Berlioz wrote **program music**. One of his most famous works *Symphonie Fantastique* was inspired by his infatuation with a Shakespearean actress he had seen perform named Harriet Smithson. He eventually married Harriet with Liszt as the witness.

Berlioz was the first virtuoso conductor. He taught orchestras and other conductors the possibilities of the orchestra. He stood in front of the musicians and interpreted the music. He taught them how to be precise in notes and rhythms, think as a group, and play with enthusiasm and vigor. Berlioz expanded the size of the orchestra to suit his wishes and the size of the hall where the performance was to take place. Berlioz did not want his audience to merely hear the music, but to vibrate with the music.

In lean times Berlioz was music critic for a Paris newspaper. He did not enjoy this job but was very good at it. He also published a book about interpreting expressiveness in music.

Berlioz's compositions were each one uniquely expressive. His music best interpreted the feelings of melancholy, yearning, reflection on nature, introspection, and the noise of crowds.

He died in 1869.

Frederic Chopin

FREDERIC CHOPIN

Frederic Chopin, born in 1810 near Warsaw, Poland, was a child prodigy and virtuoso pianist. He began piano lessons at age six and played in his first public concert at age eight.

In contrast to the fiery Berlioz and the flashy Liszt, Chopin's piano music was delicate and sophisticated. He was greatly influenced by the folk music of Poland. His **mazurkas** and **polonaises**, Polish folk dances in triple meter, displayed Chopin's **nationalistic** inspiration. He detested program music and did not compose it.

Chopin moved to Paris in 1830 where he met Liszt and Berlioz. He supported himself by teaching and composing, not by giving concerts, something he did not enjoy. His fine manners and dress made him a welcome teacher and recitalist in wealthy homes.

Chopin's musical contributions include extending the use of the piano's expressive ability in an original way, inventing innovative technical passages and fingerings, and enhancing the use of pedals. These combined to set a high standard of musical excellence in the quality of his compositions. He wrote etudes to help his students master the demands of his music.

Chopin contracted tuberculosis. Over a 10-year period, it slowly eroded his health until his death in 1849 at the age of 39.

MUSIC

QUESTIONS ABOUT COMPOSERS

What is the common element in the music of the Romantic period?

What are some of the cultural values of the Romantic period?

In what city was the cultural center of the Romantic period?

Name three composers who lived and worked in Paris during the Romantic period.

Where and when was Liszt born?

How did Liszt's compositions contribute to later music?

Franz Liszt

What is a "symphonic poem?"

Where and when was Hector Berlioz born?

How did Berlioz get his early music training?

What was different about the way Berlioz composed, compared to Chopin and Liszt?

Why did Berlioz come to Paris initially?

Frederic Chopin

66

Hector Berlioz

What did he end up studying?

_____

What type of music did Berlioz write?

_____

What is "program music?"

_____

What did Berlioz do in addition to writing music?

_____

What made Berlioz a virtuoso conductor?

_____

_____

What feelings did Berlioz's music most successfully express?

_____

_____

Where and when was Chopin born?

_____

How did Chopin receive his early music training?

_____

Describe Chopin's piano music.

_____

What are mazurkas and polonaises?

_____

Why was Chopin welcome in society homes in Paris?

_____

List Chopin's musical contributions.

_____

_____

MUSIC

Activity~

Make a chart comparing and contrasting Liszt, Berlioz, and Chopin. Be sure to include their backgrounds, styles, contributions to music, and similarities as well as differences.

Liszt	Berlioz	Chopin

Bedrich Smetana

Bedrich Smetana, a composer from Bohemia, wrote a cycle or series of six symphonic poems called *Ma Vlast* which means "My Country." This series of symphonic poems displays the nationalistic style developed by some composers in the Romantic era. This nationalistic program music describes the appearance of the countryside and incorporates its legends and history by using descriptive music and folk songs to glorify the nation of Bohemia. The most famous of these six symphonic poems is *Vltava*, or "The Mouldau," the name of the longest river in Bohemia. The music describes different scenes of life along this river.

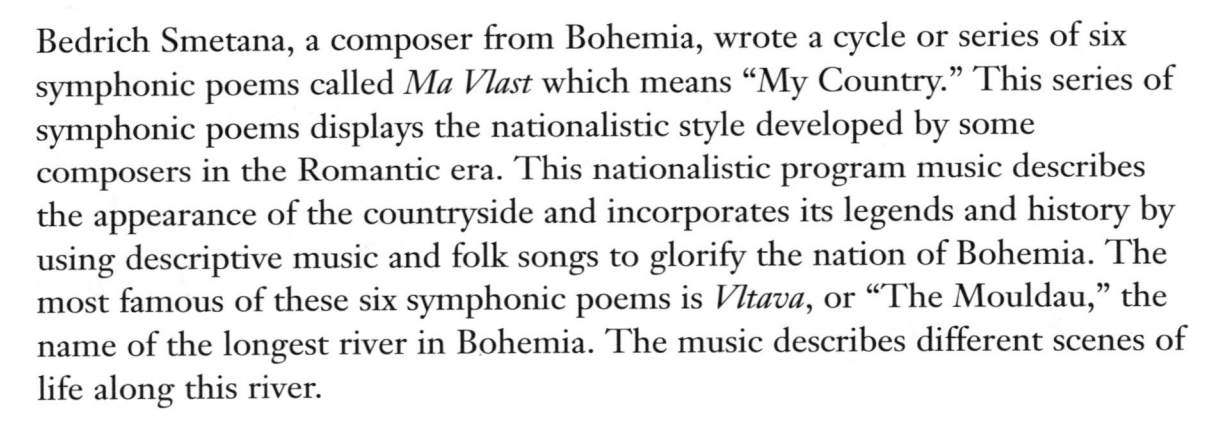

Through the music, Smetana describes two small springs arising in the forest and joining together happily in the morning sun. They move quickly until they swell into the mighty river Mouldau. The Mouldau flows through the forest where hunting horns can be heard as the hunters chase their prey through the forest. It flows through meadows where the sounds of a peasant wedding can be heard in the folk melodies of a peasant dance. At night nymphs can be heard playing in the river. Glorious deeds of long ago knights can be heard as the river passes an ancient castle. The river again emerges into rapids and flows through and past Prague by Vysehrad, an ancient fortress.

Each of these parts of the life of the Mouldau River has its own musical theme to describe it. The themes are as follows:

The Springs:

The River:

The Hunt:

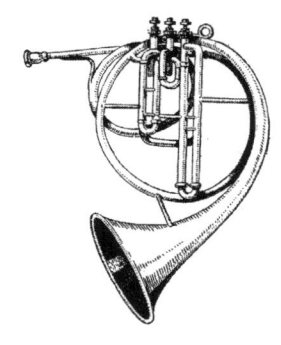

The Wedding Dance:

The Night on the River:

The Ancient Castle

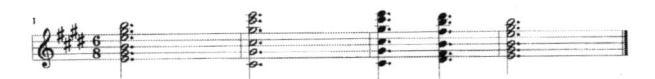

The Vysehrad, the Ancient Fortress

When the river returns, the river theme is played again.

A. Locate a copy of *The Mouldau* by Bedrich Smetana. Play these themes on a piano or find someone who can play it for you. As the music plays, listen for the themes above.

B. The music suggests many pictures. Illustrate your ideas of what the Mouldau River might look like.

MUSIC

BERLIOZ'S PROGRAM MUSIC

Symphonie Fantastique, one of Hector Berlioz's most famous works, is an excellent example of **program music**. It is loosely based on Berlioz's real life infatuation with Harriet Smithson, an actress who he later married. This work is in five movements, each describing the main character's (a man's) infatuation with his "love" in a different light.

The *idee fixe* or principal theme represents the main character's love. It appears in each movement but is altered to fit the mood or "program" of the movement.

The *idee fixe* as it appears in the first movement:

The **"program"** of the music for each movement is as follows:

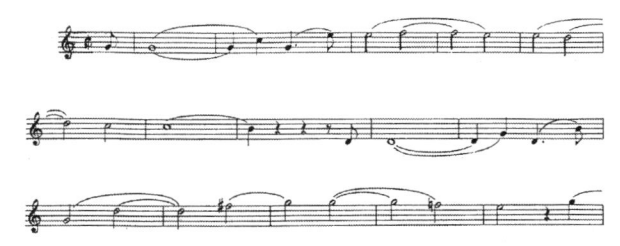

First movement: Reveries: Passions
The main character sees his "love" for the first time.
Her theme is played as he spots her and instantly falls in love.

Second movement: A Ball
This movement is a waltz in 3/4 time indicating the characters are attending a ball. As he sees her, the *idee fixe* is changed and heard played in 3/4 time.

Third movement: In the Country
This movement takes place in the country. It begins in peace and tranquility. A shepherd can be heard playing his pipe that is answered by another shepherd some distance away. The main character is disturbed by thoughts of his "love" thinking she might be deceiving him. The *idee fixe* is changed slightly and has an air of desolation. It ends with a roll of thunder, ominously foreshadowing future events.

Fourth movement: March to the Scaffold
In this movement the main character tries to kill himself. In his hallucination he dreams that he

has killed his love and is witnessing his own execution. Just before the execution, he hears the clarinet play the *idee fixe* in a forlorn way, followed by the execution. It ends with drum rolls over brass chords and moves right into the fifth movement without stopping.

Fifth movement: Dream of a Witches' Sabbath
In the fifth movement, the *idee fixe* is changed into a cackling, mocking sound as if his "love" has joined in with the witches' round dance. The *Dies irae*, medieval chant from the Catholic mass for the dead, can be heard in the low brass.

The Dies irae:

A. Locate a CD or other recording of Berlioz's *Symphonie Fantastique*. Play the *idee fixe* and the *Dies irae* on the piano or other instrument to become familiar with their sounds. Pick a movement and listen to it. Listen for the *idee fixe*. Draw a picture of the scene Berlioz is trying to show through his music.

B. List the instruments of the orchestra that you can recognize in each movement.

_____
_____
_____
_____
_____
_____
_____
_____

C. Draw and label as many of these instruments as you can.

MUSIC

73

ROMANTICISM
MATH

Mathematicians and their Countries

During the Neoclassical and the Romantic time periods, many new and exciting discoveries were being made in the scientific area of mathematics. Most of the higher math we use today was developed during this time. The mathematicians who spent their lives making these discoveries came from many different countries around the world and were different from each other in many ways. One scholar made very important contributions in many areas of math even though he was blind. Another was a female who was forced to study in hiding and submit her findings under an assumed name because women of her time were not supposed to do "brainwork."

Euler

One was a professor who invented the system of measurement most widely used around the world today. One mathematician made all of his contributions in several different areas of mathematics at a very young age. We know this is true because he was killed in a duel when he was only 21 years old. These are only a few of the famous mathematicians from this time.

In the puzzles on the following page, the countries of these famous men and women are shown along with the number of spaces in the name of the mathematician. Use the list of the names in the next excercise and see if you can match each scholar with the country.

Puzzle of Mathematicians' Countries

SWITZERLAND

FRANCE

FRANCE

GERMANY

NORWAY

FRANCE

FRANCE

ITALY

Laplace

SWITZERLAND   FRANCE

Lagrange

PRUSSIA   FRANCE

ROMANTICISM
WORD BOX

- Abel
- Cauchy
- Fourier
- Gauss
- Jacobi
- Laplace
- Bernoulli
- Euler
- Galois
- Germain
- Lagrange
- Legendre

MATH

FAMOUS MATHEMATICIANS WORD SEARCH

Now that you are more familiar with the famous mathematicians, look for their names and countries in the following puzzle. Below is the list of words you should look for.

Gauss

ROMANTICISM
WORD LIST

- Abel
- Bernoulli
- Cauchy
- Euler
- Fourier
- France
- Galois
- Gauss
- Germain
- Germany
- Italy
- Jacobi
- Lagrange
- Laplace
- Legendre
- Norway
- Prussia
- Switzerland

L	X	S	C	F	L	E	G	E	N	D	R	E	F	W
H	L	M	G	A	U	S	S	V	K	B	W	O	D	I
A	N	I	A	M	R	E	G	X	C	A	U	C	H	Y
N	O	R	W	A	Y	P	G	Q	O	R	H	H	E	G
B	A	U	J	E	R	A	I	N	I	S	E	S	C	E
G	L	W	D	M	H	U	Y	E	A	O	T	N	A	R
X	K	E	N	H	O	Z	R	N	G	R	Z	K	L	M
I	L	L	U	O	N	R	E	B	O	L	G	U	P	A
E	U	L	E	R	B	S	D	O	S	I	L	A	A	N
A	J	D	N	A	L	R	E	Z	T	I	W	S	L	Y
B	O	J	H	I	P	A	J	B	Q	H	O	O	O	D
E	C	N	A	R	F	J	A	C	O	B	I	L	W	S
L	V	I	T	A	L	Y	M	W	E	J	J	A	A	O
X	Y	Z	U	H	W	A	I	S	S	U	R	P	W	G
G	W	S	C	L	Q	N	O	S	F	V	I	F	S	Q

MATH

Leonhard Euler
1707-1783

Leonhard Euler (LAY-on-ard OY-ler) was an important mathematician of the Neoclassical time period who influenced mathematicians in the Romantic period and even those of today. He was born in Basel, Switzerland, where he grew up and attended school.

He loved to study about the sciences, especially mathematics. He spent most of his time working on solutions to some of the most challenging mathematical problems of his time. He was known for his many contributions in the areas of calculus, algebra, geometry, trigonometry, number theory, and probability. He liked showing others how mathematics played a big part in studying astronomy, artillery, navigation of ships, statistics, finance, optics, music, and mechanics.

Leonhard Euler

Euler wrote many books explaining his findings. He also loved to write textbooks. He was very good at writing them so that they were easy for students to understand. For this reason a lot of professors wanted to use his textbooks. He also created many of the mathematical symbols we use today. Although Euler is said to have written and contributed more to mathematics than any other person, he is probably more famous for another of his great accomplishments.

Activity~

To find out what else Euler is famous for, answer the following problems. Then move down to the message and fill in the missing letter wherever you find that number.

problem	answer	letter
1. 5 + 3 =	_____	A
2. 31 - 11 =	_____	B
3. 25 x 3 =	_____	C
4. 3 + 8 + 10 =	_____	D
5. (3 + 2) x (8 - 3) =	_____	E
6. 15 - 8 =	_____	F
7. 6 x 7 =	_____	I
8. 12 - 3 =	_____	K
9. 10 x 10 =	_____	L
10. 100 - 50 =	_____	M
11. (4 x 2) - 8 =	_____	N
12. (2 x 8) - 1 =	_____	O
13. 20 + 7 =	_____	R
14. (5 + 3) x 2 =	_____	S
15. (15 - 3) + 6 =	_____	T
16. 66 - 33 =	_____	W
17. (20 - 7) x 2 =	_____	Y

He __ __ __   __ __ __ __ of his __ __ __ __
   21 42 21   50 15 16 18   20 25 16 18

__ __ __ __   __ __ __ __ __   he __ __ __ __ __ __
33 15 27 9   8 7 18 25 27   20 25 75 8 50 25

__ __ __ __   __ __ __ __ __ __   in 1766.
18 15 18 8   100 100 26   20 100 42 0 21

MATH

79

DRIVEN BY A PURE LOVE OF MATHEMATICS

Sophie Germain (zhair - MAN) (1776-1831) loved to read and study _____ (7 letters). She was very interested in learning about _____ (11 letters). It wasn't easy for Sophie to find a chance to study for she had to do it in secret.

During her lifetime it was believed that _____ (8 letters) or "brainwork" was not good for _____ (5 letters). People thought that it was unhealthy and maybe even _____ (9 letters). So, because Sophie was a female, she was not allowed to attend _____ (6 letters). Only boys could go to school to learn. Her parents saw how interested she was in mathematics, so they let her study in _____ (7 letters) at home using their large _____ (7 letters) of books. She had to promise them that she would stop studying if she started to feel _____ (3 letters).

Sophie learned of a new school the _____ (5 letters) _____ (14 letters) that was to open in _____ (5 letters) and have only the best professors. Then she became sad because she knew that only _____ (4 letters) would be allowed to attend. However, she decided that this would not stop her. With the help of a _____ (7 letters), she was able to submit papers to _____ (9 letters) Lagrange, who taught at the school. She submitted these papers under the assumed name of "_____ (8 letters) LeBlanc." _____ (8 letters) was so impressed with her work that he asked to meet with this student in person. When he was told that this _____ (7 letters) was a female, he was shocked, but he still wanted to meet her. He was very _____ (10 letters) of her _____ (4 letters).

Laplace

80

Later _____ became interested in learning about the_____ of
     6 letters   6 letters

mathematics. She was especially interested in mathematician_____Gauss'
                                                              4 letters

contributions to this_____. Soon she started corresponding with _____
                       6 letters   5 letters

still using the assumed name "Monsieur_____". Before long Carl Gauss
                                        7 letters

learned of Sophie's true _____. Gauss was so impressed with her _____
                           8 letters   5 letters

that he passed her _____ on to his fellow colleagues.
                              15 letters

Sophie gained _____ recognition in 1816 when she developed her
                5 letters

theory on elastic surfaces. This theory helped _____ many
                                                  5 letters

_____ problems of her time. One _____ building that was
     12 letters   6 letters

constructed using her law of vibrating _____ surfaces was the
                                          7 letters

_____Tower.
 6 letters

Sophie_____may have lived during a time when_____were
       7 letters   5 letters

not thought to be as strong as men, but she did not let anything or anyone

stop her from _____all she could about mathematics.
                8 letters

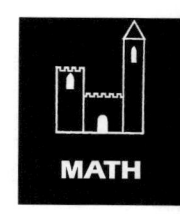

Gauss

81

Use the words in the lists below to fill in the blanks of the story "Driven By a Pure Love of Mathematics." Find the correct word to fill in each blank by matching the letter number clues with an appropriate word from the columns below.

3 letters
ill

4 letters
boys
Carl
work

5 letters
Gauss
girls
ideas
Paris
solve
women
world

6 letters
Eiffel
famous
female
friend
school
Sophie
theory

7 letters
elastic
Germain
LaBlanc
library
private
science

8 letters
identity
Lagrange
Monsieur
studying
learning

9 letters
dangerous
Professor

10 letters
interested
supportive

11 letters
mathematics

12 letters
construction

15 letters
accomplishments

(2 words)
(5 letters + 14 letters)
Ecole Polytechinique

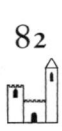

82

Famous Neoclassical and Romantic Era Mathematicians — Timeline

Daniel Bernoulli (1700–1782) Switzerland
Bernoulli was from a distinguished family of mathematicians in Switzerland that spanned six generations and over 200 years. In probability theory he is best known for his distinction between mathematical expectation and "moral" expectation.

Leonard Euler (1707–1783) Switzerland
Euler, more than any other mathematician, was responsible for the form and notation of college level mathematics that we use today.

Louis Lagrange (1736–1813) Italy
Lagrange was responsible for France adopting the metric system of weights and measures in 1799.

Pierre-Simon Laplace (1749–1827) France
Laplace contributed more to the theory of probability than any other mathematician.

Adrien-Marie Legendre (1752–1833) France
Legendre wrote a geometry textbook that dominated the teaching of geometry in America until 1850.

Jean-Baptiste Fourier (1768–1830) France
Fourier proved that any function $y = f(x)$ can be represented by a special series using trigonometric functions now known as a Fourier series.

Sophie Germain (1776–1831) France
Sophie was awarded a prize from the Paris Academy of Sciences for her work on the mathematical theory of elastic surfaces.

Carl Friedrich Gauss (1777–1855) Germany
Gauss was the greatest German mathematician of the 19th century. He was a child prodigy and is best remembered for his method of summing the numbers from 1 to 100 in his head when he was only ten years old.

Augustin-Louis Cauchy (1789–1857) France
Cauchy was the first person to prove one of Fermat's most difficult theorems. This theorem states that each positive integer is the sum of at most three triangular numbers or four square numbers or five pentagonal numbers, and on and on . . .

Niels Henrik Abel (1802–1829) Norway
Two days after Abel died of tuberculosis at the age of 27, a letter arrived offering him a math position in Berlin. He never knew of the interest in his work with polynomial functions which was published just prior to his death.

Carl Gustov Jacobi (1804–1851) Prussia
Jacobi developed several theorems related to elliptic functions.

Evariste Galois (1812–1832) France
Galois was killed in a duel at age 20. At such a young age, he had already made many important discoveries in the field of algebra. Most were not published until after his death.

Activity~

Make a list of mathematicians and their contributions to math.

Mathematician's name	Contribution
_____	_____
_____	_____
_____	_____
_____	_____
_____	_____
_____	_____
_____	_____
_____	_____

LAGRANGE AND THE METRIC SYSTEM

Joseph Louis Lagrange (zho-SEF loo-EE la-GRAHNZH) (1736 – 1813) was a French physicist and mathematician who helped to found two academies of science and was partially responsible for and contributed to the use of the metric system.

Lagrange had a way of making difficult mathematical ideas seem easy.

Lagrange

He convinced the members of the French Units and Measures Committee to use the base 10 as a standard for their system, rather than 12 as the Egyptians and Greeks had done. Twelve had long been considered a superior number, but to Lagrange moving the decimal point to change from one unit to another seemed much easier.

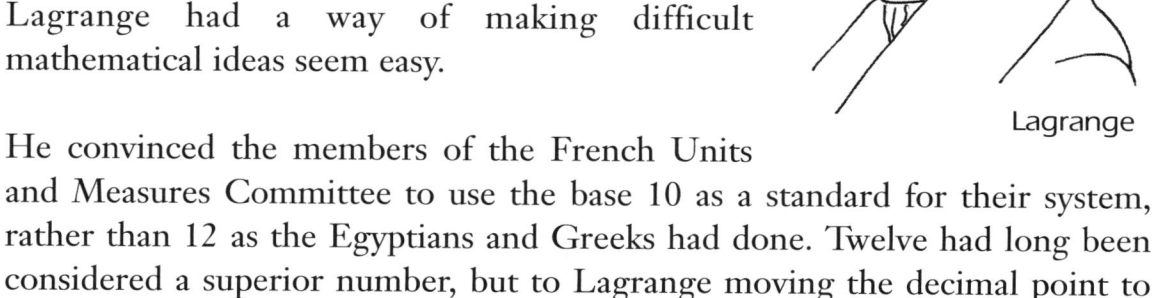

Look at the following to see why Lagrange considered the metric system simpler to use.

12 inches = 1 foot
3 feet = 1 yard
1,760 yards = 1 mile

To convert miles to feet you must multiply by 1,760, then by 3, and then by the number of miles you are converting. 1 mile = 1,760 yards/mile x 3 feet/yard x 1 mile = 5,280 feet. 4 miles = 1,760 yards/mile x 3 feet/ yard x 4 miles = 21,120 feet.

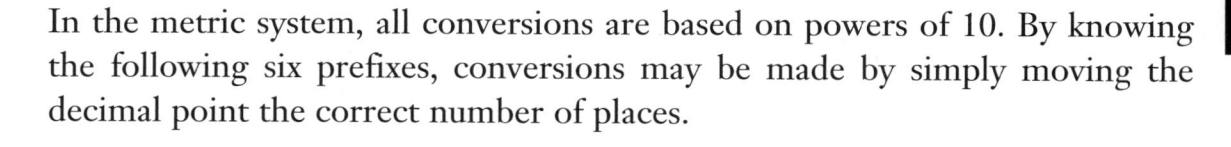

In the metric system, all conversions are based on powers of 10. By knowing the following six prefixes, conversions may be made by simply moving the decimal point the correct number of places.

Prefix	Meaning
milli-	one-thousandth (1/1,000)
centi-	one-hundredth (1/100)
deci-	one-tenth (1/10)
deka-	ten (10)
hecto-	one-hundred (100)
kilo-	one-thousand (1,000)

MATH

Notice: 1600 millimeters = 160.0 centimeters = 16.00 decimeters = 1.600 meters.

If we are referring to the metric unit of distance, the meter, then 1 millimeter is 1/1000 of a meter and 1 kilometer is 1000 meters. There are three basic units all using the same prefixes. We have discussed the meter as the unit for distance. The unit for volume is the liter and for mass it is the gram.

Abbreviations are simple, too. They are not capitalized and do not use periods. Here are some common metric abbreviations. See if you can recognize a pattern and fill in the blanks.

Metric Name	Abbreviation
Meter	m
Liter	l
1. _____	g
millimeter	mm
milliliter	ml
milligram	2. _____
centimeter	cm
decimeter	dm
deciliter	3. _____
4. _____	dg
kilometer	km
5. _____	kl
kilogram	kg

Here are a few common equalities:

1,000 ml = 1 l   3,000 m = 3 km
10 cm = 1 dm   10 dm = 1 m
2,000 g = 2 kg   4,000 mg = 4 g

Now it is your turn. See how well you do on the following matching quiz.

Answers: 1. gram; 2. mg; 3. dl; 4. decigram; 5. kiloliter

METRIC MATCHING QUIZ

MATCH EACH NUMBER TO THE APPROPRIATE LETTER.

(Ans)

(H)	1. The prefix kilo- means	A.	one-tenth (1/10)
(F)	2. 1000 m =	B.	dm
(M)	3. The abbreviation for millimeter	C.	one-hundred (100)
(L)	4. 2 cm =	D.	4 m
(A)	5. The prefix deci- means	E.	1000 l
(T)	6. The abbreviation for liter	F.	1 km
(N)	7. The abbreviation for kilogram	G.	the liter
(Q)	8. The abbreviation for meter	H.	one-thousand (1000)
(O)	9. 2000 mg =	I.	2 m
(J)	10. The prefix milli- means	J.	one-thousandth (1/1000)
(E)	11. 1 kl =	K.	one-hundredth (1/100)
(R)	12. 3000 g =	L.	20 mm
(K)	13. the prefix centi- means	M.	mm
(G)	14. The metric unit of volume	N.	kg
(I)	15. 200 cm =	O.	2 g
(C)	16. The prefix hecto- means	P.	the gram
(B)	17. The abbreviation for decimeter	Q.	m
(P)	18. The metric unit of mass	R.	3 kg
(D)	19. 4000 mm =	S.	ten (10)
(S)	20. The prefix deka- means	T.	l

Carl Friedrich Gauss
1777-1855

GAUSS: A GREAT MATHEMATICIAN

Carl Friedrich Gauss (1777 – 1855) is said to be the greatest German mathematician of the 19th century. He was a child prodigy.

When he was only ten, Gauss' teacher gave the class a math problem that was supposed to take a long time. The problem was to sum the numbers from 1 to 100. Carl did the problem immediately in his head and got the correct answer, 5050. How was Carl able to do this problem so quickly?

Gauss

Consider the following. First, write the sums across your paper once forward and once backward, like this.

1	+	2	+	3	+	...	+	98	+	99	+	100
100	+	99	+	98	+	...	+	3	+	2	+	1
101	+	101	+	101	+	...	+	101	+	101	+	101

Notice that summing down, each pair of numbers adds to 101. 1 + 100 = 101, 2 + 99 = 101, 3 + 98 = 101, etc. How many pairs are we summing? _____ (100). So, multiply 100 times 101 to get 10,100. But this answer includes summing the numbers from 1 to 100 twice. Therefore, to get the answer to our problem we must divide by two. Thus, the sum of the numbers from 1 to 100 is 10,100 ÷ 2 = **5,050**.

Now, you find the answers to the following sums by using Gauss' method. Add the first number to the last number. Multiply by the number of terms and divide your answer by two. We refer to these sums as Gaussian sums.

1. Find the sum of the numbers from 1 to 50. (1,275)
2. Find the sum of the numbers from 50 to 150. (10,000)
3. Find the sum of the numbers from 1 to 200. (20,100)
4. Find the sum of the odd numbers from 1 to 99.
   Hint: Use the same method as above. Just remember there are only half as many terms; i.e., multiply by 50. (2,500)
5. Find the sum of the even numbers from 2 to 100. (2,550)

Two Mathematicians from the Romantic Age

Find the names of two mathematical geniuses whose lives were cut short in the Romantic age. One lived from 1802 until 1829, and the other lived from 1812 until 1832. First, calculate the value of the number expressions to get the number for each letter below. Then, write the letter that goes with each number in the puzzle spaces (puzzle is on next page). After the letters are all filled in, the two words reading **across** will spell the name of one mathematician and how he died at the age of 20. The two words reading **down** give the name of another mathematician and how he died at the age of 27.

Number Expression	Value in Simplest Form	Letter
$(4/3) \div (4/15)$	_____	A
$10°$	_____	B
$3\,2/3 + 2\,1/3$	_____	C
$1{,}000 - 991$	_____	D
$28/14$	_____	E
$3^2 + 3$	_____	G
$\sqrt{25} - \sqrt{4}$	_____	I
5×1.4	_____	L
$1/100$ of $1{,}000$	_____	O
$(13 \times 45) \div 45$	_____	R
$1{,}001 \div (7 \times 13)$	_____	S
$\sqrt{16}$	_____	T
2^3	_____	U

(Answers: A=5, B=1, C=6, D=9, E=2, G=12, I=3, L=7, O=10, R=13, S=11, T=4, U=8)

Romantic Age Mathematicians Puzzle

								4
								8
								1
								2
								13
								6
								8
								7
								10
		12	5	7	10	3		11
			1					3
			2					11
9	8	2	7					

(Answers: Across—Galois, Duel   Down—Abel, Tuberculosis)

90

EARLY NINETEENTH CENTURY COMPUTER HISTORY

Joseph Jacquard (1752–1834), a French weaver, invented an early version of his loom for weaving cloth in 1801. Each design change had to be carried out by a human operator. In 1805 Jacquard perfected his loom by using punched cards as a method of controlling the operation of the loom. He did not have computers in mind, but his idea of storing information on punched cards was later used in early computers.

Charles Babbage (1792–1871), an Englishman, is known as the Father of Computers. In 1822 he designed the Difference Engine for calculating logarithms and trigonometric functions. He finally abandoned it because there was no technology to build parts based on his design.

Later in 1832, he designed a multi-purpose computer he called the Analytical Engine. Babbage planned for his new computer to receive numerical instructions or input in the form of punched cards. It would process and store information and print out the final results. The Analytical Engine had all four parts of a modern day computer – input, output, memory, and a central processing unit. Babbage was so far ahead of his time that people had a hard time understanding him and called him "eccentric."

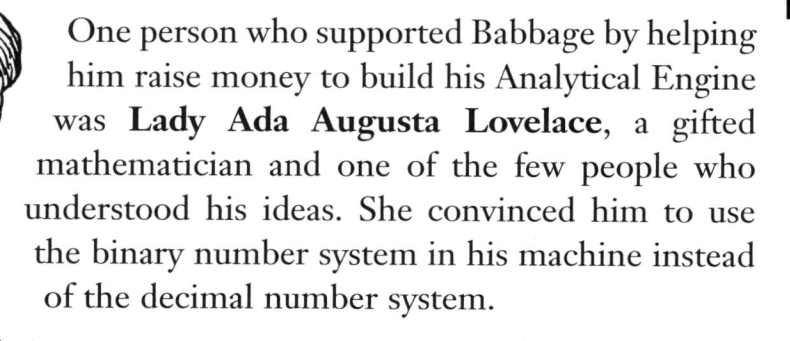

One person who supported Babbage by helping him raise money to build his Analytical Engine was **Lady Ada Augusta Lovelace**, a gifted mathematician and one of the few people who understood his ideas. She convinced him to use the binary number system in his machine instead of the decimal number system.

None of the mechanical tools of Babbage's time were precise enough to build his complicated machine, nor was electricity even used. Unfortunately, the Analytical Engine never worked and Babbage died thinking he had been a failure. More than 100 years later, Babbage's ideas were used in the first "modern" computer. This is why today he is called the Father of Computers.

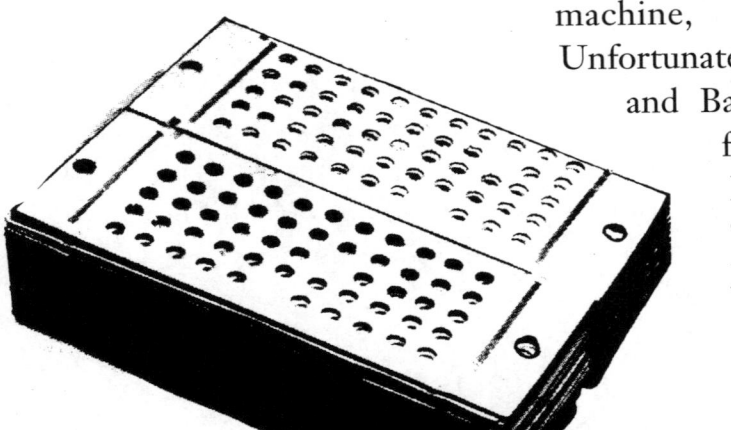

Be a computer designer. Tell what important features your computer of the 21st century will have. Draw a picture to help explain your ideas.

MATH

COMPUTER HISTORY QUESTIONS

1. What idea for putting information into his Analytical Engine did Babbage borrow from the French weaver Jacquard? _____
   _____
   _____

2. How was the Analytical Engine similar to a modern day computer?
   _____
   _____
   _____

3. What important contribution did Lady Ada Augusta Lovelace make to the Analytical Engine? _____
   _____
   _____

4. It is sometimes said that Babbage was born in the wrong century. Do you agree or disagree? Why? _____
   _____
   _____

MATH

ROMANTICISM
SCIENCE

R.T. Laennec
1781-1826

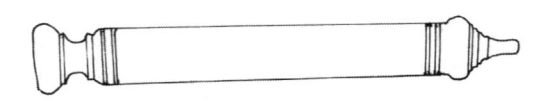

Laennec invented the monaural (one-ear) **stethoscope** in 1816. The first ones he used were rolled up paper. Later he used wooden cylinders. The new stethoscopes helped the sounds of the heart and lungs become clearer to the listening doctor. They probably saved Dr. Laennec and his patients much embarrassment because before using the stethoscope he had to listen by putting his ear directly on the patient's chest! The stethoscope was improved in 1852 when bendable tubing became available and two ear pieces were used.

QUESTIONS:

1. What does monaural mean? _____

2. What do you think binaural means? _____

3. How were the first monaural stethoscopes made? _____

Activity~

Materials: a piece of notebook paper and a paper-towel cardboard tube

Try listening to another student's heart using your first monaural stethoscope — the paper rolled into a cylinder. Then listen through the cardboard tube. Try to listen to breathing also. Trade places and repeat. Record your findings below:

_____
_____
_____

Ignaz Semmelweis
1818-1865

The Hungarian doctor Ignaz Semmelweis (1818-1865) was one of the first people to notice the connection between dirt and disease. At about the same time, Dr. Gordon from Scotland and Dr. Oliver Wendell Holmes were also working on this connection. In 1846 Dr. Semmelweis noted that in the obstetrics unit (where babies are born) in a hospital in Vienna, Austria, a large number (10% to 30%) of women died from blood poisoning after birth. In another obstetrics unit in the same hospital, the death rate of mothers was much lower. What was the difference? In the first unit, doctors and medical students cared for the women. Often they had just dissected a body, examined a patient who was ill, or checked another pregnant woman. They went from person to person without washing their hands. On the second unit, midwives cared for the women and delivered their babies. The midwives almost always washed their hands between patients and always washed between deliveries.

Semmelweis ordered hand washing with a disinfectant and by 1848 the death rate was lowered to only 1%.

QUESTIONS:

1. What three doctors were noting the connection between filth and either disease or death? _____

2. What observation did Semmelweis make about the two obstetrics units? _____

3. What was the outcome of his observation? _____

Activity~

Materials: Mix a box of Jello according to directions and pour into 4 containers (containers you could throw away are best). You will also need Saran wrap, paper and a pencil. Label your containers 1-4.

Container 1: do nothing but cover with Saran wrap.
Container 2: cough on the Jello and cover.
Container 3: wash hands thoroughly, touch Jello, and cover.
Container 4: wipe your hands across the table, over books, pencils, and other objects—touch the Jello and cover.

Do not uncover the Jello containers. Place all containers somewhere safe in a room. Observe each day for 7 to 10 days and record. At the end of the activity, ask an adult to help you throw away the Jello.

Container	1	2	3	4
Day 1				
Day 2				
Day 3				
Day 4				
Day 5				
Day 6				
Day 7				
Day 8				
Day 9				
Day 10				

SCIENCE

ROMANTIC INVENTIONS

STEAM LOCOMOTIVES

Train engines, called locomotives, were first invented during the early 1800s. The first train engines, like you see in the picture, were called steam locomotives. They burned coal to produce heat which turned water into steam. The steam created pressure which turned the wheels of the engine. During the 19th century, inventors were constantly improving the steam locomotive to make it bigger and stronger so that it could travel longer distances and pull more train cars.

Many people in the 19th century thought the steam locomotive was a great invention. Romantics, however, did not like their modern world of machines, factories, and cities. Romantics yearned for the quiet countryside undisturbed by noisy trains.

Pretend that you think trains are a terrific invention.

1. What animal is the steam locomotive like and why? _____
   _____

2. What shape is the steam locomotive like and why? _____
   _____

3. What color is the steam locomotive like and why? _____
   _____

4. Now pick your favorite description above—either animal, shape, or color. Pick more words that complete this description.

   Nouns:_____
   Verbs: _____
   Adjectives: _____

SCIENCE

Pretend that you are a Romantic and think trains are a terrible invention.

5. What animal is the steam locomotive like and why? _____
_____

6. What shape is the steam locomotive like and why? _____
_____

7. What color is the steam locomotive like and why? _____
_____

8. Now pick your favorite description above—either animal, shape, or color. Pick more words that complete this description.

Nouns: _____
_____

Verbs: _____
_____

Adjectives: _____
_____

9. Now write about the advantages and disadvantages of trains. Use words from your lists of ideas above. Continue this paragraph on another page.

_____
_____
_____
_____
_____
_____
_____
_____

SCIENCE

RESPONSES TO GREAT INVENTIONS

Activity~

The dates, names, events, or inventions are true but the quotations are guaranteed to be completely fallacious. Create your own ridiculous quotations on the blank lines.

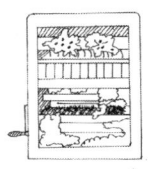

1. "Are cotton seeds that much trouble?"
   1792 Eli Whitney: Cotton gin

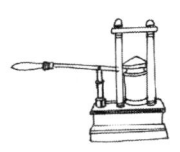

2. "We're going to get these things together."
   1796 – Joseph Bramah: Hydraulic Press

3. "This little needle won't hurt a bit."
   1796 – Edward Jenner: smallpox vaccination

4. "You are going to do what with that rock?"
   1798 – Alois Senefelder: Lithography

5. "Take that rock out of the kitchen."
   1799 – Rosetta Stone is found.

6. "This should light up things."
   1800 – Alessandro Volta: Battery

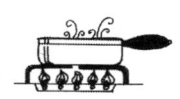

7. "I am so tired of chopping and carrying wood."
   1802 – Zachaus Andreas Winzler: Gas stove

SCIENCE

8. "You spent how much for a swamp?"
   1803 – United States buys Louisiana territory from France

9. "There will never be any use for this thing."
   1803 – Richard Trevithick: Railway locomotive

10. "But Bonaparte, I am the Pope. I am supposed to crown you."
    1804 – Napoleon Bonaparte crowns himself emperor of France, the "New Rome"

11. "Yeah, but who's going to turn them on and off?"
    1807 – Gas street lighting

12. "Wow, now we can have Spam!"
    1811 – Nicholas Appert: Canned food

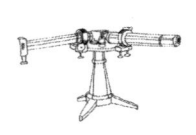

13. "Somewhere over the rainbow, bluebirds fly."
    1814 – Joseph von Frauenhofer: Spectroscope to study spectrum of sunlight

14. "Cool, Davy, cool."
    1815 – Humphry Davy: Miner's safety lamp

15. "Every beat of my heart is for you."
    1816 – Rene Laennec: Stethoscope

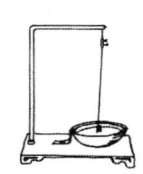

16. "People will always prefer steam."
    1821 – Michael Faraday: Electric motor

SCIENCE

17. "It's about time. Richard made that locomotive back in 1805."
    1825 – First railroad

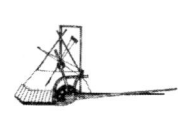

18. "This doesn't have anything to do with the Grim Reaper, does it?"
    1826 – Patrick Bell: Reaping machine

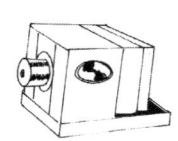

19. "I don't see much use for it."
    1827 – Joseph-Nicephore Niepce, Louis Daguerre: Photography

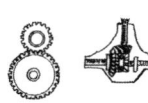

20. "If you could just invent a car, maybe those gears would be useful."
    1827 – Onesiphore Pecqueur: Differential gears

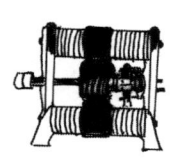

21. "I am a dynamo!"
    1831 – Michael Faraday: Dynamo to produce electricity

22. "Now maybe I'll get to work on time."
    1839 – Kirkpatrick Macmillan: Bicycle

23. "I want the self-sticking kind with roses on them."
    1840 – James Chalmers, Rowland Hill: Postage stamp

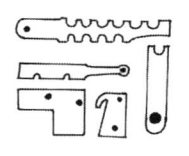

24. "Parts of what?"
    1840 – Marc Brunel: Interchangeable parts manufacture

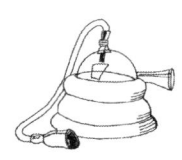

25. "I can't feel a thing."
    1844 – Horace Wells: Anesthetics

SCIENCE

101

26. "I came on frequent flyer miles."
    1847 – California gold rush
    _____

27. "I thought about going into painting with that artist Seurat."
    1844 – Samuel Morse: Morse code
    _____

28. "I'm sorry to hear that your tires are sick, Mr. Thomson."
    1845 – R.W. Thomson: Pneumatic tires
    _____

29. "Cut out the noise."
    1846 – Antoine Sax: Saxophone
    _____

Draw some of your ideas for inventions.

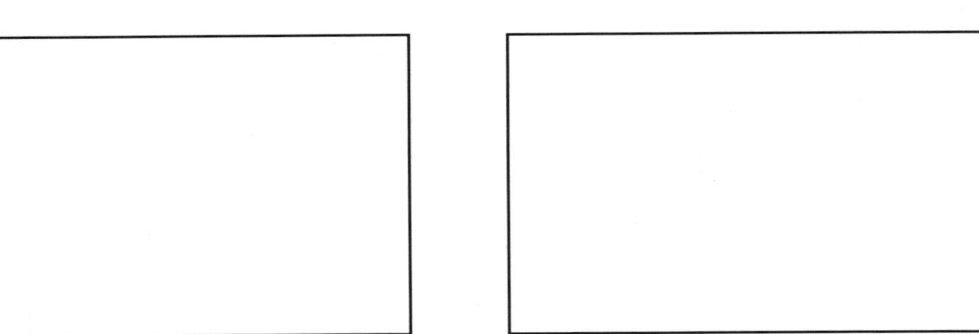

INVENTIONS, DISCOVERIES AND EVENTS MATCH

1. ___ Antoine Sax
2. ___ Humphry Davy
3. ___ Eli Whitney
4. ___ R.W. Thomson
5. ___ Joseph Bramah
6. ___ Rene Laennec
7. ___ Edward Jenner
8. ___ Zachaus Andreas Winzler
9. ___ Nicolas Appert
10. ___ Michael Faraday
11. ___ Samuel Morse
12. ___ Joseph von Frauenhofer
13. ___ Alois Senefelder
14. ___ Napolean Bonaparte
15. ___ Richard Trevithick
16. ___ Alessandro Volta
17. ___ Patrick Bell
18. ___ Louis Daguerre
19. ___ James Chalmers
20. ___ Horace Wells
21. ___ Onesiphore Pecqueur
22. ___ Marc Brunel
23. ___ Kirkpatrick Macmillan
24. ___ Rowland Hill
25. ___ Joseph-Nicephore that Niepce

A. invented cotton gin
B. invented hydraulic press
C. discovered how a vaccination could prevent illness
D. developed the process lithography
E. invented the battery
F. developed the gas stove
G. invented the railroad locomotive
H. crowned himself emperor of France
I. invented the process where food could be canned
J. invented spectroscope
K. produced a safety lamp for miners
L. invented stethoscope
M. invented electric motor and dynamo
N. Scotsman who invented reaping machine
O. invented photography
P. perfected the Daguerreotype Photographic Process
Q. invented the differential gear used in automobiles
R. invented bicycle
S. suggested the use of gummed postage stamps
T. started the low cost uniformly priced postage stamp service
U. pioneered the process of manufacturing interchangeable parts
V. developed "laughing gas" as an anesthetic
W. developed system of sending letters in a code of dots and dashes
X. introduced the pneumatic(inflated) tire
Y. patented an instrument made of brass created sound with vibrating reeds

answers: 1.Y, 2.K, 3.A, 4.X, 5.B, 6.L, 7.C, 8.F, 9.I, 10.M, 11.W, 12.J, 13.D, 14.H, 15.G, 16.E, 17.N, 18.P, 19.S, 20.V, 21.Q, 22.U, 23.R, 24.T, 25.O

SCIENCE

ROMANTICISM REVIEW

ROMANTIC PERIOD TIMELINE

Use the information from the Quick Facts section or any other resource you wish to create your own **Romantic period timeline**. Select a variety of famous people and famous events. Put in birth and death dates for people like the one below. Color or decorate the horizontal strip in some way that reminds you of the person or event.

	1750	1760	1770	1780	1790	1800	1810	1820	1830	1840	1850

Goya   1746   1848
Spanish artist

ROMANTIC EVALUATION

In this unit you have learned about artists and their artwork, inventors and their inventions, and famous architecture built during this era. Use your productive thinking skills to choose your favorites.

1. One of my favorite inventions from this time period is the _____
_____

   It was invented by _____

   It was used to _____

2. One of my favorite paintings from this unit was _____
_____

   The artist who did this work was _____

   It shows _____

3. A work of architecture I learned about was _____

   It is located in _____

   Some of its features are _____
_____

4. A famous person from this period is _____

   This person was famous for _____

5. If I had lived in the Romantic time, I would have been

   a _____

   and _____

105

Letters Home

You have just completed an adventure through the exciting, turbulent Romantic era. Write a letter home telling about your experiences. Be sure to make it imaginative and creative. Write with deep feeling.

Date_____

Dear_____,

_____
_____
_____
_____
_____
_____
_____
_____

With deep emotion,

_____

Create an emotional, exciting illustration to accompany your letter.

REVIEW

ROMANTICISM
TIMELINE REVIEW

See pages 6 and 7.

Time Period _____

Characteristics _____
_____
_____
_____

Time Period _____

Characteristics _____
_____
_____
_____

ROMANTICISM
TIMELINE REVIEW

See pages 6 and 7.

REVIEW

Time Period _____

Characteristics _____

_____

_____

_____

Time Period _____

Characteristics _____

_____

_____

_____

109

ROMANTICISM
TIMELINE REVIEW

See pages 6 and 7.

Time Period _____

Characteristics _____
_____
_____
_____

Time Period _____

Characteristics _____
_____
_____
_____

110

BIBLIOGRAPHY FOR ROMANTIC ERA

Burns, Edward. *Western Civilizations*. Norton.
Canaday, John. *Mainstreams of Modern Art*. Holt, Rinehart, Winston.
Clark, Judith. *History of Art*. Mallard Press.
Clark, Kenneth. *Civilisation*. Harper and Row.
Cole, Bruce and Adelheid Gealt. *Art of the Western World*. Summit Books.
Dorra, Henri. *Art in Perspective*. Harcourt Brace Jovanovich.
Eyewitness Science - Medicine. Dorling Kindersley.
Fradin, D. B. *Medicine, Yesterday, Today, and Tomorrow*. Children's Press.
Garder, Helen. *Art Through the Ages*. Harcourt Brace Jovanovich.
Hollingsworth, Patricia and Stephen Hollingsworth. *Smart Art*. Zephyr Press.
Hone, E., et al. *A Sourcebook for Elementary Teachers*. Harcourt, Brace, and World.
Illustrated Encyclopedia of Western Art. Exter Books.
Jacobs, Jay. *Encyclopedia of World Art*. Octopus Books.
Janson, H. W. *History of Art*. Prentice Hall.
Platt, Richard. *Smithsonian Visual Timeline of Inventions*. Dorling Kindersley.
Schlichter, Carol. *Talents Unlimited in Renzulli's Systems and Models*. Creative Learning.
Steves, Rick and Gene Openshaw. *Europe 101*. John Muir Publications.
Strickland, Carol and John Boswell. *The Annotated Mona Lisa*. Universal Press.
Sutcliffe, J. and N. Duin. *A History of Medicine*. Barnes and Noble.
Timetables of Science. Simon and Schuster.
Timetables of History. Simon and Schuster.
Turvey, Peter. *Timelines Inventions*. Franklin Watts.
Wallis, Frank. *Ribbons of Time*. Weidenfeld and Nicolson.
Winters, Nathan. *Architecture is Elementary*. Gibbs Smith Publisher.

SAILS
History of Architecture

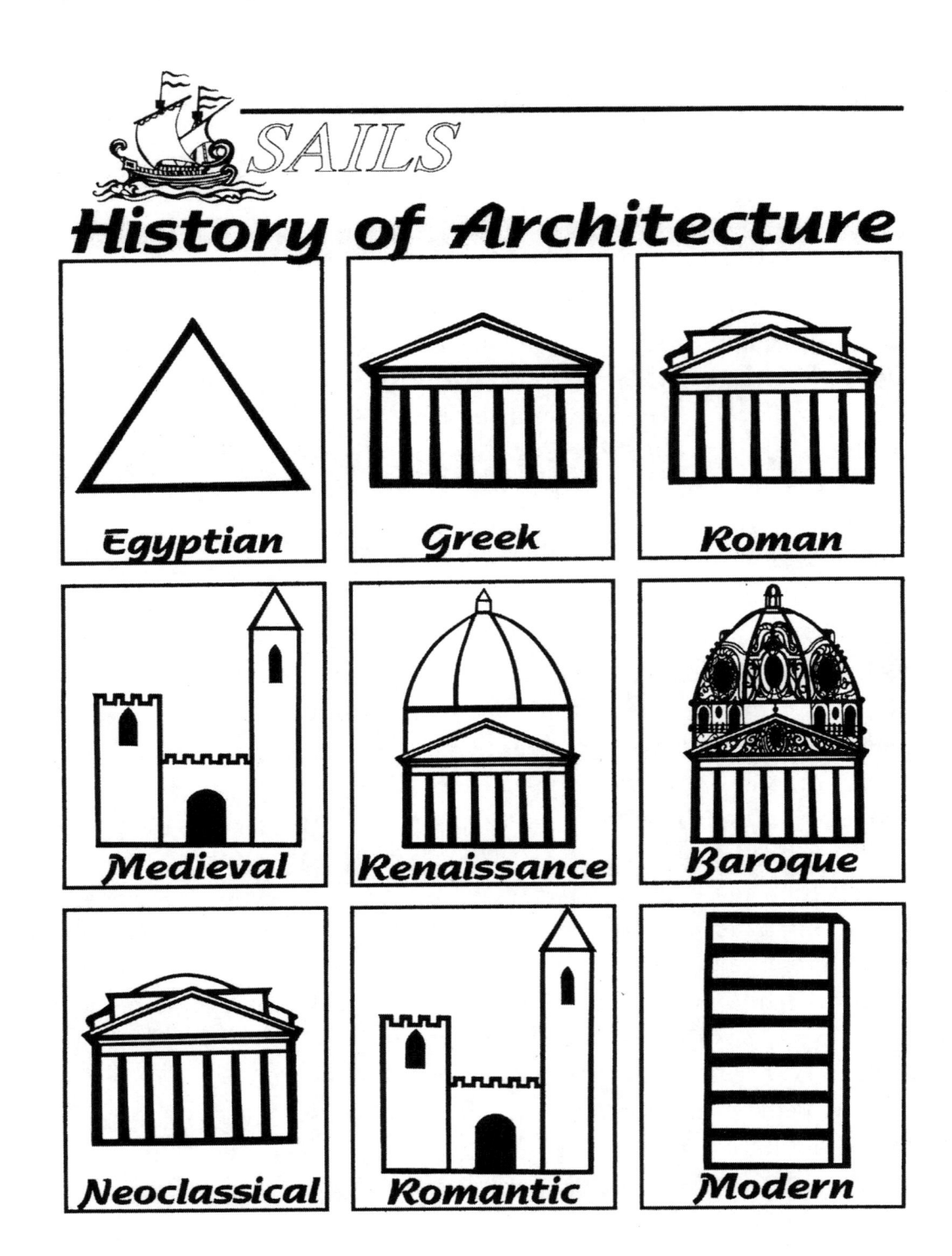

Egyptian	Greek	Roman
Medieval	Renaissance	Baroque
Neoclassical	Romantic	Modern

To order t-shirts with the above design or to receive additional information regarding SAILS History of Architecture Series contact:

University School at The University of Tulsa
800 South Tucker Drive, Tulsa, Oklahoma 74104
Phone: 918-631-5060   Fax: 918-631-5065
Visit: 326 South College Avenue, Tulsa, Oklahoma 74104
e-mail: debra-price@utulsa.edu